Children's Literature for the Primary Inclusive Classroom

CHILDREN'S LITERATURE FOR THE PRIMARY INCLUSIVE CLASSROOM

by

Nancy D'Isa Turner, Ed.D.
Saint Mary's College
Notre Dame, IN

MaryAnn Traxler, Ph.D.
Saint Mary's College
Notre Dame, IN

Delmar
Thomson Learning™

Africa • Australia • Canada • Denmark • Japan • Mexico • New Zealand • Philippines
Puerto Rico • Singapore • Spain • United Kingdom • United States

NOTICE TO THE READER

Publisher does not warrant or guarantee any of the products described herein or perform any independent analysis in connection with any of the product information contained herein. Publisher does not assume, and expressly disclaims, any obligation to obtain and include information other than that provided to it by the manufacturer.

The reader is expressly warned to consider and adopt all safety precautions that might be indicated by the activities herein and to avoid all potential hazards. By following the instructions contained herein, the reader willingly assumes all risks in connection with such instructions.

The Publisher makes no representation or warranties of any kind, including but not limited to, the warranties of fitness for particular purpose or merchantability, nor are any such representations implied with respect to the material set forth herein, and the publisher takes no responsibility with respect to such material. The publisher shall not be liable for any special, consequential, or exemplary damages resulting, in whole or part, from the readers' use of, or reliance upon, this material.

Delmar Staff:
BusinessUnit Director: Susan Simpfenderfer
Acquisitions Editor: Erin O'Connor-Traylor
Development Editor: Melissa Riveglia
Editorial Assistant: Alexis Ferraro
Executive Marketing Manager: Donna Lewis
Executive Production Manager: Wendy Troeger
Production Editor: Suzanne Nelson

Cover Design: TerraLuma Design, Cathleen Berry

Library of Congress Cataloging-in-Publication Data
Turner, Nancy D'Isa.
    Children's literature for the primary inclusive classroom / by Nancy D'Isa Turner, Mary Ann Traxler.
        p. cm.
    Includes bibliographical references and index.
    ISBN 0-7668-0345-7
    1. Handicapped children—Education (Primary)—United States. 2. Children's literature—Study and teaching (Primary)—United States. 3. Inclusive education—United States. I. Traxler, Mary Ann Duranczyk. II. Title.
    LC4028.T87   2000
371.9'0446—dc21   99-21304
                                                                                                                CIP

With affection to my children—
    Katie, for her good nature and outstanding creativity;
    Erin, for her amazing energy and passion; and
    Jacob, for his curiosity and zest for life.
    To my husband, Jay, for his unfailing patience.

                  N. Turner

To my children with love—
    Nikolas, for his intensity, caring concern, and
    wonderful conversations.
    Elizabeth, for her love of learning and generous spirit.
    Alex, for his persistence and sense of adventure.
    Emily, for her incredible energy and warm snuggles.

                  M. Traxler

CONTENTS

PREFACE

During the 1992-93 school year, the authors of this book conducted a study involving two midwestern school districts implementing their first year of full inclusion of students with moderate to severe mental and/or physical disabilities. Parents of children with disabilities as well as teachers of general education classrooms including these students were surveyed as to the concerns, successes, and challenges of the program. Principals were personally interviewed. Most were very positive about the experience, however, one issue that arose involved promoting an understanding of the children with disabilities among those without disabilities. Teachers felt a need to facilitate this understanding, and some weren't sure at that time just how to go about it.

With this discovery, the authors conceived the idea for this text as a "teacher-friendly" resource wherein teachers from grades kindergarten through three could easily access titles and descriptions of children's literature featuring children with a variety of disabilities. In this text, books in various genres which include children with disabilities as a primary or secondary character have been selected and are summarized. Disability categories follow those outlined by the Individuals with Disabilities Education Act (IDEA), and include physical disabilities, hearing impairment, mental retardation, visual impairment, learning disabilities, other health impairment, serious emotional disturbance, autism, speech and language impairment, and multiple disabilities. (The authors could not locate books about another category under IDEA, traumatic brain injury.) In addition, a chapter on literature about children with Attention-Deficit Hyperactivity Disorder, although not included as a separate category under IDEA, is included in this text. It was felt that the potential opportunity for teachers to readily access books on this topic warranted a separate chapter. This organizational system for the text is, admittedly, categorical, even though many school districts are moving to a more cross-categorical programming model. It must be stated that in spite of this organization (which appeared to the authors to be the easiest to utilize) and resultant use of the books, teachers must guard against reinforcing any stereotypes that typically come to mind with the categories of disabling conditions presented. The diversity not only among categories, but within each category, must be emphasized.

It is envisioned that teachers in an inclusive setting or even a more restrictive setting can utilize this book to easily access quality children's literature about this topic. It could also be used by child care providers for before- and after- school care. The books can be read to (or by) children in either large or small group situations to encourage an understanding of various disabling conditions. This reading is valuable as a stand-alone activity or as part of a unit on valuing and respecting differences. Many schools are attempting to build a more multicultural and/or thematic curriculum; this text could be one means to aid in this endeavor.

While a simple reading of books is a valuable activity in itself, extension of the children's experiences through various activities is integral to promotion of some of the values and attitudes the authors espouse. To help teachers in their planning, activities which are designed to help all students gain insights into themselves and others follow each book summary and include discussion, writing, art, drama, music, and research. Teacher-initiated activities, indicated first under the summary, are designated with an icon, while student-directed activities follow with no special designation. The authors have attempted to make these activities as "hands-on" as possible. Most of them can be done with minimal cost and with ordinary classroom/school supplies.

No specific criteria have been applied for selection of the books. Any known recognition that the book has been given (for example, awards or honors) is identified in the summary. Given the expertise of classroom teachers, their knowledge of their individual students, and the research information provided, teachers will be able to make judgments concerning appropriate literature choices and related activities.

ACKNOWLEDGMENTS

We owe a debt of gratitude to many individuals who have helped with the development of this book. It would not have been written without the conversations and discussions with teachers, parents, and principals involved in our initial study of inclusion. We would like to thank the reference staff from the Cushwa-Leighton Library at Saint Mary's College, especially Jill Hobgood and students Stacey Curtis and Anna Knapp who obtained many of the children's books for us through interlibrary loan. The staff of the St. Joseph County Public Library System also located many of the books for this project. We would like to thank our colleague, Dale Banks, for sharing his computer expertise and also our student assistants Sarah Dunn, Sarah Thieneman, and Nikki Hoevet, for word processing the initial manuscript and for their patience through the many revisions and last-minute insertions. We greatly appreciate Dr. Frank D'Isa (father of Nancy Turner) and Curt Traxler for their skills in photographing the books and children in some of the pictures; likewise, we thank the teachers who allowed us into their classrooms to take pictures and the children and the adults who agreed to be photographed. Several children provided their work and projects as photographed examples, and we feel these are a wonderful addition to our activities sections. We also appreciate the publishers and authors who permitted us to photograph the covers of their books and offered complimentary copies of books we might find interesting. The mini-grant awarded by the Indiana Association of Teacher Educators also enabled us to personally own many of the children's books. A number of these books and activities have been used by our college students in field study placements; we are grateful for their willingness to try out some of our ideas and provide helpful feedback, as well as contribute lesson plans for one of the appendices. We appreciate the words of encouragement, help, and patience from the editors and staff of Delmar Publishers, and the staff of Argosy, for editing and typesetting the book efficiently and diligently. The support from colleagues (Karilee Freeberg, Loretta Li, and Minerva Straman) and students in the Education Department at Saint Mary's has likewise been valuable. We are grateful for the conference support offered by Saint Mary's, providing an opportunity to share our findings and gather ideas from professional colleagues across the country. Ultimately, we could not have completed this book without the support and love of our families:

I want to especially thank my children, Katie, Erin, and Jacob, for their patience and understanding when mom was always working on "the book;" my parents, Frank and Mary Kay D'Isa, for their words of encouragement and helpful suggestions; my sister Janie and other family members, for their pride in my work; and most of all my husband Jay, who is always there for me with great advice and support.

N. Turner

I greatly appreciate the support of my family during the writing of this book. I could not have done this without the encouragement and creative scheduling of my husband, Curt. Lots of hugs also to my children, Nikolas, Elizabeth. Alex, and Emily for giving up some time with me and taking care of each other. A special thank you to Elizabeth for her interest in this project and for her contributions.

M. Traxler

Special appreciation is due to the reviewers involved in the development of the text.

Linda Aiken
Southwestern Community College
Sylva, NC

David Anderson, Ed.D.
Bethel College
Dallas, TX

Margot Heller
Lima Technical College
Lima, OH

Melinda Lindsay, Ph.D.
Boise State University
Boise, ID

Diana Marsh
Kenai Peninsula College
Soldotna, AK

Jill Stanton
University of Wisconsin - Stout
Menomonie, WI

Terry Weaver, Ph.D.
Union University
Jackson, TN

ABOUT THE AUTHORS

Nancy D'Isa Turner is an associate professor of education at Saint Mary's College, Notre Dame, Indiana. She received a Doctor of Education degree in 1992 from Andrews University, Berrien Springs, Michigan, a Master's degree from Youngstown State University in 1982, and a Bachelor's degree from Bowling Green State University in 1978.

Dr. Turner teaches undergraduate courses in corrective reading methods, strategies for exceptional learners, and multicultural education, as well as supervises student teachers. She teaches graduate courses in curriculum and instruction. Dr. Turner presents at state and national conferences on topics related to reading methods and successful inclusion strategies. She has authored several articles related to these topics.

MaryAnn Traxler is an associate professor of education at Saint Mary's College, Notre Dame, Indiana. She received a Ph.D. in Education from Michigan State University in 1983, a Master's degree from Central Michigan University in 1973, and a Bachelor's degree from Michigan State University in 1972.

Dr. Traxler supervises student teachers and teaches undergraduate courses in developmental reading methods, children's literature, and multicultural education. She also established the Saint Mary's College Reading Center that connects children in need of reading assistance with undergraduate students. Dr. Traxler presents at state and national conferences on topics related to reading and whole language. She has authored several articles particularly related to the inclusion of children with disabilities in children's literature.

CHAPTER 1

INTRODUCTION
AND BACKGROUND

HISTORICAL PERSPECTIVE

Total educational segregation of students with disabilities is for the most part, a thing of the past. With the passage of the Education for All Handicapped Children Act (P.L. 94-142) in 1975, children with disabilities have had a right to a free and appropriate public education in the least restrictive environment (U.S. Department of Education, 1997). Interpretation of the "least restrictive environment" concept has been central to the development of programs over the years.

Special education programs were initially categorical types organized around the disabilities recognized by P.L. 94-142: learning disability, mental retardation, seriously emotionally disturbed, communication disorders, visual impairment, hearing impairment, deafness-blindness, orthopedic impairments, other health impairments, and multiple disabilities. These narrowly framed programs identified "factors thought to predispose students to poor learning ability" (Wang, Reynolds, & Walberg, 1994–95, p. 13), and delivered instruction specific to the remediation of these factors. When students had demonstrated a level of proficiency deemed adequate, they were mainstreamed into the general education classroom for "regular" instruction. Both the special educator and the general educator instructed the students according to their respective responsibilities as delineated in an individualized education program (IEP).

Philosophically, special education and general education became two distinct entities. Teacher training for special and general education teachers took on different focuses. Special education teachers examined behavior management, diagnosis and prescription for learning deficiencies, and techniques for working with unconventional learners, whereas general educators prepared in the academic disciplines—composition, literature, mathematics,

1

science, and so on (Yatvin, 1995). Each group had its area of expertise, supposedly neither overlapping nor understood by the other. In the school setting, special education teachers were often viewed as "recipients of students sent to them rather than partners with other teachers" (Goodlad, 1993, p. 4) in the planning for the education of all students.

This dual system of service delivery did not always yield the benefits originally planned. Some research within the last fifteen years on the efficacy of segregated special education programs does not support this option. On the contrary, it has shown that students with disabilities benefit from placement in general education settings where interactions with students who are not disabled are common (Brimer, 1990; Halvorsen & Sailor, 1990; McDonnell, Wilcox, & Hardman, 1991; Meyer, Peck, & Brown, 1991). There is clear support for integrated, less restrictive environments.

Several factors have influenced the development of integrated programs. The Regular Education Initiative was a movement among educators in the late 1980s that promoted the merger of special and general education (Lloyd, Singh, & Repp, 1991). According to Stainback, Stainback, and Bunch (1989), the purpose of the initiative "was to find ways to serve students classified as having mild and moderate disabilities in regular classrooms by encouraging special education and other special programs to form a partnership with regular education" (p.11).

Public Law 101-476, the Individuals with Disabilities Education Act (IDEA), is the 1990 amendment to P.L. 94-142. IDEA expanded the notion of the least restrictive environment to include alternative placements such as home instruction, hospitals, and institutions that would meet the needs of students. While still mandating a "continuum of services" (for example, resource rooms, self-contained classrooms, and general education classrooms) for students with disabilities, it provided the language for full inclusion as a legitimate option. "It may be inferred that Congress intended the IDEA to spur an overall restructuring of school systems so that students with severe disabilities would be educated within the general education setting" (Osborne, DiMattiv, & Curran, 1994, p. 12). (It should be noted that IDEA made other changes to the original law, such as adding autism and traumatic brain injury to the categories eligible for special services, and mandating transition services for students beginning at age 16).

In 1997, the Act was reauthorized again as P.L. 105-17, the Individuals with Disabilities Education Act Amendments of 1997 (IDEA 97). The new law made several changes to the 1990 amendments. One change deals with assessment; if a child's disability has not changed over a three-year period, he or she should not be subjected to unnecessary reassessment to determine continued eligibility for special education. Another change focuses on discipline;

the law explicitly requires appropriate help for children who need instruction in and services for following rules and getting along in school. In addition, if a child is removed from school for behavioral reasons, the child must be allowed to participate in the general curriculum and receive designated services/modifications in the alternative setting. IDEA 97 strengthens the role of parents by mandating their participation in decision making about eligibility and placement. General education teachers must now be a part of the IEP team. Schools are required to assume greater responsibility for ensuring that students with disabilities have access to the general education curriculum, and to delineate how modifications in instruction and administration of assessments will be made. Finally, the new law allows IDEA-funded staff, who work in general education classrooms with children with disabilities, to work with others who may need their help as well. There are other changes made by IDEA 97 that focus on younger and older children; however, those cited previously are specific to children in the elementary grades (cited in Heumann & Hehir, 1997).

WHAT IS INCLUSION?

The term "full inclusion" describes the placement of children with disabilities in a general education classroom with children who do not have disabilities. Sometimes the concepts of mainstreaming and inclusion are confused.

> Inclusion differs from mainstreaming in that the latter integrates students with disabilities into the regular school program mainly through peripheral programs, such as physical education or the arts. Students are still the responsibility of a special education teacher. In inclusion, students with disabilities are in regular classrooms and are the *responsibilities* of the regular teacher. (Lewis, 1994, p. 71)

Putnam, Spiegel, and Bruinks (1995) stated that "a growing number of schools and entire districts educate nearly all students in general classrooms rather than pullout classrooms" (p. 553).

According to Smelter, Rasch, and Yudewitz (1994), inclusionists philosophically believe that children learn best in the general education classroom, that inclusion answers the call for social equity among students, and that integration is a moral and ethical right of every individual, regardless of the disability. Although these are general beliefs of those who espouse inclusion, different factions within this group of proponents appear in the literature: those who advocate the total elimination of special educators while the general educator takes full responsibility, and others who support a restructuring with the special educator and paraprofessional working with the general education teacher and going into the general education classroom to instruct the student with disabilities (and possibly students without disabilities) (Fuchs & Fuchs, 1994–95). The authors of this book endorse the latter interpretation of inclusion—that full supports must be in place for the students to function optimally in the general education classrooms.

IMPLICATIONS OF INCLUSION: THE DISTRICT AND SCHOOL

The question of the extent to which students with disabilities should be included is being debated in school districts across the country. Many related issues directly impact or are affected by the decision to include. Three factors that must be addressed by the school or district are: outcomes and accountability for these students, the costs of inclusion, and the effects of inclusion on learning.

According to Ysseldyke, Thurlow, and Shriner (1992), all educators will be asked at some point to provide evidence of the progress or lack of progress that students are making toward the goals, outcomes, or standards established as necessary for improving education in America. This standards-based reform focuses on *all* students, including those for whom expectations have been traditionally low; it also calls for a heavy reliance on achievement testing. However, the National Research Council (1997) indicated that many states and local school districts are keeping students with disabilities out of their accountability systems because of fears that they pull down scores. What can be done to alleviate these concerns? Shriner, Ysseldyke, Thurlow, and Honetschlager (1994) suggested "an alternative assessment system to measure the performance of students who do not take part in the regular assessment" (p. 39). Others (O'Day & Smith, 1993) emphasized that the standards movement must respond to student differences. IDEA 97 requires that a student's IEP explain any modifications in the administration of state- or district-wide assessments that are needed so that the child can participate (cited in Hardman, Drew, & Egan, 1999). Although progress is being made, the issue clearly must be addressed by those considering inclusion.

Is inclusion cost effective for school districts? If done correctly, inclusion is not a money-saving option for a school or district. As stated previously, no support services should be taken away from the student (and in fact, even more might be added). In addition, all members of the inclusion team need extensive training in working with students in the classroom (VanDyke, Stallings, & Colley, 1995). This training is integral to the success of an inclusion program. Staff development must be intensive and continuous and must focus on outcomes/accountability issues, as well as appropriate curriculum and instructional adaptations. Anything less constitutes irresponsible planning and teaching.

Most important, programs must examine the effects on students' learning and social relationships as a result of inclusion. As mentioned earlier, research within the last fifteen years has indicated that segregated special education programs have not yielded the expected results for students with disabilities. Three meta-analyses address the issue of the most effective settings for the education of these students, comparing inclusive and noninclusive environments (Baker, 1994; Carlberg & Kavale, 1980; Wang & Baker, 1985–86). These studies "demonstrate a small-to-moderate beneficial effect of inclusive education on the academic and social outcomes of special needs children" (cited in Baker, Wang, & Walberg, 1994–95, p. 34). In addition, significant gains in acceptance of those with disabilities among those without disabilities occur when the level of contact is high (Favazza & Odom, 1997). The effects of inclusion on the academic and social abilities of students with disabilities appears to be positive and worthwhile.

Likewise, several studies indicate that there are generally no adverse effects on the academic achievement of students without disabilities when educated in inclusive classrooms. Bricker, Bruder, and Bailey (1982) tracked the developmental progress of children without disabilities enrolled in integrated preschool programs including children with disabilities over one or more years and found no evidence of developmental harm. Cooke, Ruskus, Apollini, and Peck (1981) compared the progress of matched groups of children without disabilities in inclusive and noninclusive classrooms on standardized measures of cognitive, language, and social development, and found no significant differences in development. In a study of full-inclusion programs in school districts across four states, Morra (1994) found that for students without disabilities, "parents and teachers perceived them becoming generally more compassionate, more helpful, and more friendly in relating to . . . students [with disabilities]" (p. 1). These are but three examples of studies with positive results.

IMPLICATIONS OF INCLUSION: THE CLASSROOM

What skills must the general education teacher have in order to meet the demands of an inclusive classroom? To be successful in an inclusive setting, a general education teacher must believe that all students can learn; expectations for students cannot be lowered. All members of the class must feel that they are equal members of the classroom community and that their needs can and will be met. Effective discipline strategies must be in place for all students. This entails realistic goals for the behavior of students and the means to aid in the realization of these goals.

Instructional strategies that are effective for students without disabilities are often effective for students with disabilities. These include such strategies as cooperative learning and thematic instruction. Putnam et al. (1995) proposed more holistic/constructivist teaching strategies, such as whole language and outcome-based assessment, for inclusive classrooms. Such methods enable the learner to construct meaning in the context of his or her own knowledge. Greater individualization can take place when support personnel work with all students in the class in addition to working with students with disabilities (Logan, Bakeman, & Keefe, 1997). General education teachers must be aware of curricular and instructional modifications, such as adaptations in instructional activities and materials (for example, clarifying or shortening task directions); modifications in teaching procedures (for example, changing the pace of instruction); changes in task requirements (for example, breaking each task into smaller tasks); and choice of alternative task selection (for example, selecting a similar, but easier task from the same or different curriculum) (Idol & West, 1993).

CONNECTIONS TO CHILDREN'S LITERATURE

Helping students with disabilities assimilate in the regular classroom may appear to be the teacher's primary challenge. Developing awareness and improving the attitudes of children without disabilities toward children with disabilities, however, have become major concerns for educators, particularly those in states choosing or mandating the inclusion of children with disabilities in the regular classroom. Hopkins (1980) discussed a study done by Monson and Shurtleff (1979) that found that children who read or listened to books about disabilities showed the greatest positive attitude change toward people with disabilities.

Dobo (1982) concluded that education needs to produce both cognitive and affective change concerning children with disabilities. Nonfiction and informational books can provide accurate information about the causes, treatment, and equipment related to a disability. In addition, affective change involves understanding "the way handicapped people view themselves, the challenges they meet, and how they react to often difficult situations" (p. 292). Ferguson (1981, pp. 8–9) suggested that children's literature can contribute to the "growth of a more compassionate and humanistic person." Reading and discussing books that include children with disabilities allow children to experience empathy. A vicarious experience through a story can provide an opportunity for children to accept someone with a disability, recognize their feelings, and respect people who are different.

According to Crook and Plaskon in 1980, reading stories with children that include children with disabilities, followed by thoughtful discussion, can assist a teacher in determining her students' thoughts and feelings about disabilities and those experiencing them (cited in Dobo, 1982). A number of trade books featuring children with disabilities are available and suitable for use at home and in classrooms. Though some books are about children with disabilities, others are compelling stories that happen to focus on a child with disabilities. Huck, Hepler, and Hickman (1997, p. 475) suggested that good stories about children with physical disabilities serve two purposes: to provide positive images with which the child with disabilities may identify, and to help children without disabilities "develop a more intelligent understanding of some of the problems that disabled persons face."

Trade books, used for instructional purposes or for pleasure, can provide valuable information about children with disabilities and according to Hopkins (1980), can be used in several ways. Becoming familiar and comfortable with children with disabilities promotes more positive attitudes on the part of children without disabilities. A child with disabilities may have an opportunity to identify with a book character who also has a disability. Finally, books about children with disabilities may simply be good stories. Lass and Bromfield (1981) agreed that stocking the classroom library with books about children with disabilities broadens students' awareness and helps teachers and students become attuned to students with disabilities.

In her writing about children with learning disabilities, Gold (1983) maintained that it is critical to provide opportunities for children to develop their self-esteem and to help other children understand and be sensitive to related problems. Sharing children's literature can provide positive images with which children with disabilities can identify. Through characters encountered in books, many children learn about themselves, clarify some of their ideas and concerns, and develop stronger self images.

Quicke (1985, p.5) felt that fiction, in particular, can provide "a total picture of the experience of disability in the context of a story which captures the imagination of the reader." Children who listen to or read the story can become a part of it and begin to understand disability in social and emotional contexts. "The author may choose, for example, to see the world through the young eyes of a child with special needs or a sibling or a friend of such a child, and in doing so manage to convey a sense of the complexity of their psychology—the confusions, contradictions, likes and dislikes, feelings about other people's attitudes, frustrations, hopes, fears, etc."

In an analysis of characteristics of children's literature including people with disabilities, Hopkins (1980) found that most books written for children were most often written about an individual child with one type of disability rather than multiple disabilities. Further, she points out that most recent books emphasize the positive outlook on life and the great gains that these individuals with disabilities have made despite their condition. Those with disabilities are realistically portrayed as productive members of society who contribute much to the lives of their families and friends. Following an examination of children's literature portraying children with disabilities before and after 1978, Harrill, Loung, McKeag, and Price (1993) noted that there are more books including children with disabilities and a greater variety of disabilities portrayed in children's literature after 1978. They also found that the text and illustrations of their post-1978 sample were much more realistic. The books published after 1978 also provided more accurate information and terminology than their predecessors.

Reflecting on literature about children with disabilities, Cullinan asserted, "Literature provides a measuring stick for some; a portrait of another's life dominated by a disability for the rest. It enables all of us to share another's distress and celebrate the unconquerable joy in life" (1989, p. 424).

LITERATURE SELECTION

Experts in the field of children's literature have suggested various criteria for the selection of literature including children with disabilities. Norton (1999) maintained that well-written books help children without disabilities empathize with and understand children with disabilities. She also recommended using the following criteria established by Sage in 1977:

1.   The author should deal with the physical, practical, and emotional manifestations of the disabling condition accurately but not didactically.
2.   Other characters in the story should behave realistically as they relate to the individual with disabilities.
3.   The story should provide honest and workable information about disabling conditions and the potential of individuals with disabilities.

Norton further pointed out that conflict resolution can be a special concern in realistic fiction. If there is a happy ending, is it contrived or does it come about naturally and honestly? Huck, Hepler, and Hickman (1997) felt that it is especially important that stories including characters with disabilities be well written. They should not be sentimental or "evoke pity for what children with disabilities cannot do, but respect for what they *can* do" (p. 476). They further contended that characters should be multidimensional persons with real feelings and frustrations. Both the text and the illustrations should be honest in their portrayal of disabilities.

Lass and Bromfield (1981) submitted that using the following selection criteria promotes a positive, nonstereotyped view of people with disabilities. Literature should:

1.   Promote empathy rather than pity.
2.   Portray the person with the disability as human rather than romanticized.
3.   Describe admiration and acceptance rather than ridicule.
4.   Present an accurate portrayal of the behaviors associated with a specific disability.
5.   Be judged interesting for a designated age group in plot, characterization, and language.
6.   Present the child with the disability in a realistic setting when possible.
7.   Emphasize similarities rather than differences between children, both with and without disabilities.

Rudman (1995) offered additional criteria. She maintained that people with disabilities should appear as major and minor characters in about the same proportion as they occur in real life. As with other characters, they should also be multiculturally diverse and fully dimensional with similar strengths, problems, and feelings. It is also important that they be represented in various genres. Further, she felt that heroism on the part of a character with disabilities should not be a requirement for acceptance. Children with disabilities are children first—they're happy, sad, upset, frustrated, excited, fearful, loving—as all children are.

Clearly, books about children with disabilities must provide accurate information. Quicke (1985) noted that official labeling should be done correctly and treatment and equipment should be described accurately. He suggests several questions that teachers may wish to consider when selecting appropriate literature:

- Is the book basically pessimistic or optimistic?

- How is the character with the disability portrayed?

- How does the book deal with prejudice, discrimination, and role stereotyping in society generally?

- How does the book deal with social and psychological change in childhood and adolescence?

Experiences with literature provide opportunities for children to view the world from various perspectives and to grow and develop in many ways. An understanding of challenges faced by those with disabilities can be ascertained through interesting and creative use of this type of literature in the classroom.

REFERENCES

Baker, E. T. (1994). Meta-analytic evidence for noninclusive education practices: Does educational research support current practice for special needs students? Doctoral dissertation, Temple University, Philadelphia.

Baker, E. T., Wang, M. C., & Walberg, H. J. (1994-95). The effects of inclusion in learning. *Educational Leadership, 52*(4), 33–35.

Bricker, D. D., Bruder, M. B., & Bailey, E. (1982). Developmental integration of preschool children. *Analysis and Intervention in Developmental Disabilities, 2,* 207–222.

Brimer, R. W. (1990). *Students with severe disabilities: Current perspectives and practices.* Mountain View: CA: Mayfield.

Carlberg, C., & Kavale, K. (1980). The efficacy of special versus regular class placement for exceptional children: A meta-analysis. *Journal of Special Education, 14,* 295–309.

Cooke, T. P., Ruskus, J.A. Apolloni, T., & Peck, C. A. (1981). Handicapped preschool children in the mainstream: Background, outcomes, and clinical suggestions. *Topics in Early Childhood Special Education, 1*(1), 73–83.

Cullinan, B. E. (1989). *Literature and the child.* Fort Worth, TX: Harcourt Brace Jovanovich College Publishers.

Dobo, P. J. (1982). Using literature to change attitudes towards the handicapped. *The Reading Teacher, 36,* 290–292.

Favazza, P. C., & Odom, S. L. (1997). Promoting positive attitudes of kindergarten-age children toward people with disabilities. *Exceptional Children, 63*(3), 405–418.

Ferguson, A. M. (1981). *Children's Literature—For All Handicapped Children,* ERIC Document Reproduction Service Number ED234541.

Fuchs, D., & Fuchs, L. S. (1994–95). Sometimes separate is better. *Educational Leadership, 52*(4), 22–26.

Gold, J. T. (1983). "THAT'S ME!" The LD child in literature. *Academic Therapy, 18*(5), 609–617.

Goodlad, J. I., & Lovitt, T. C. (1993). *Integrating general and special education.* New York: Merrill Publishing.

Halvorsen, A. T., & Sailor, W. (1990). Integration of students with severe and profound disabilities: A review of research. In R. Gaylord-Ross (ed.), *Issues and Research in Special Education* (pp.110–172). New York: Teachers College Press.

Hardman, M. L., Drew, C.T., Egan, M. W. (1999). *Human exceptionality: Society, school, and family.* Boston: Allyn and Bacon.

Harrill, J. L., Loung, J. J., McKeag, R. A., & Price, J. *Portrayal of Handicapped/ Disabled Individuals in Children's Literature: Before and After Public Law,* ERIC Document Reproduction Service Number ED357557.

Heumann, J. E. & Hehir, T. (1997). Believing in children—A great IDEA for the future. *Exceptional Parent, 27*(9), 38–42.

Hopkins, C. J. Developing positive attitudes toward the handicapped through children's books. *Elementary School Journal, 81* (Sept. 1980), 34–37.

Huck, C. S., Hepler, S., Hickman, J. & Kiefer, B. Z. (1997). *Children's literature in the elementary school.* Madison, WI: Brown & Benchmark Publishers.

Idol, L., West, J. F. (1993). Effective instruction of difficult-to-teach students. Austin, Texas: Pro-ed.

Lass, B., & Bromfield, M. (1981). Books about children with special needs: An annotated bibliography. *The Reading Teacher, 34,* 530–533.

Lewis, A. C. (1994). Washington seen. *Educational Digest, 60*(1), 69–72.

Lloyd, J. W., Singh, N. N., & Repp, A. C. (1991). The Regular Education Initiative: Alternative perspectives on concepts, issues, and models. Sycamore, IL: Sycamore Press.

Logan, K. R., Bakeman, R., & Keefe, E. B. (1997). Effects of instructional variables on engaged behavior of students with disabilities in general education classrooms. *Exceptional Children, 63*(4), 481–497.

McDonnell, J., Wilcox, B., & Hardman, M. L. (1991). *Secondary progress for students with developmental disabilities.* Boston: Allyn & Bacon.

Meyer, L. H., Peck, C. A., & Brown, L. (ed.) (1991). *Critical issues in the lives of people with severe disabilities.* Baltimore: Paul H. Brooks.

Morra, L. G. (1994, April 28). Districts grapple with inclusionprograms. Testimony before the U.S. House of Representatives on Special Education Reform. Washington, DC: U.S. General Accounting Office.

National Research Council (1999). Educating one and all: Students with disabilities and standards-based reform. Washington, DC: National Acadamy Press.

Norton, D. E. (1995). *Through the eyes of a child: An introduction to children's literature*. Upper Saddle River, New Jersey: Merrill Publishing.

O'Day, J. A., & Smith, M. S. (1993). Systemic reform and educational opportunity. In S. H. Fuhrman (ed.), Designing coherent education policy (pp. 250–313). San Francisco, CA: Jossey-Bass.

Osborne, A. G., DiMattia, P. (1994). The IDEA's least restrictive environment mandate: Legal implications. *Exceptional Children, 61*(1), 6–14.

Putnam, J. W., Spiegel, A. N., & Bruininks, R. H. (1995). Future directions in education and inclusion of students with disabilities: A Delphi investigation. *Exceptional Children, 61*(6), 553–576.

Quicke, J. (1985). *Disability in modern children's fiction*. Cambridge, MA: Brookline Publishing.

Rudman, M. K. (1995). *Children's literature: An issues approach*. New York: Longman Publishing.

Shriner, J. G., Ysseldyke, J. E., Thurlow, M. L., & Honetschlager, D. (1994). "All" means "all"—Including students with disabilities. *Educational Leadership, 51*(6), 38–42.

Smelter, R. W., Rasch, B. W., & Yudewitz, G. J. (1994). Thinking of inclusion for all special needs students? Better think again. *Phi Delta Kappan, 76*(1), 35–38.

Stainback, W., Stainback, S., & Bunch, G. (1989). Introduction and historical background. In S. Stainback, W. Stainback, and M. Forest (eds.), *Educating all students in the mainstream of regular education*. (pp. 3–14). Baltimore: Paul H. Brooks.

U.S. Department of Education (1997). Nineteenth annual report to Congress on the implementation of the Individuals with Disabilities Education Act. Washington,DC: U.S. Government Printing Office.

VanDyke, R., Stallings, M. A., & Colley, K. (1995). How to build an inclusive school community. *Phi Delta Kappan, 76*(6), 475–479.

Wang, M. C. & Baker, E. T. (1985–1986). Mainstreaming programs: Design features and effects. *The Journal of Special Education, 19*, 503–521.

Wang, M. C., Reynolds, M. C., & Walberg, H. J. (1994–95). Serving students at the margins. *Educational Leadership, 52*(4), 12–17.

Yatvin, J. (1995). Flawed assumptions. *Phi Delta Kappan, 76*(6), 482–485.

Ysseldyke, J. E., Thurlow, M. L., & Shriner, J. G. (1992). Outcomes are for special educators too. *Teaching Exceptional Children, 25*(1), 36–50.

CHAPTER 2

LITERATURE ABOUT CHILDREN WITH PHYSICAL DISABILITIES

The Individuals with Disabilities Education Act (IDEA) uses the term "orthopedically impaired" to describe children with physical disabilities. There are many types of physically disabling conditions, including neurological conditions (cerebral palsy, spina bifida, epilepsy), muscular skeletal conditions (muscular dystrophy, juvenile rheumatoid arthritis, congenital malformation), and traumatic injury (spinal cord injuries)

According to the Nineteenth Annual Report to Congress on the Implementation of the Individuals with Disabilities Education Act (1997), approximately 63,200 children between the ages of six and twenty-one are physically disabled—one percent of the total number of children with disabilities.

The implications of a physical disability in the classroom vary, depending upon the type and severity of the condition. In many instances, mobility is of major concern. Although the passage of the Americans with Disabilities Act in 1990 required accessibility to public facilities and buildings, sometimes play equipment, furniture, or educational equipment remains inaccessible. Carpeting, rugs, or other uneven floor surfaces can pose difficulties for students in wheelchairs or for those using other assistive devices for walking (Lewis & Doorlag, 1987). Teachers and aides must be aware of guidelines for picking up and carrying students with disabilities. In addition, since assistance in eating, drinking, and using the bathroom is often required, appropriate health maintenance skills must be applied. These issues also have important implications in the context of field trips: teachers must check ahead of time on the conditions of the visiting site. Transportation may also present challenges.

Communication is also a problem for students with physical disabilities. A congenital disability or one with gradual onset can cause an inability to communicate through conventional means. This lack of communication often masks the intellectual abilities of the student. Although mental disabilities sometimes occur concomitantly with physical disabilities, "in most instances, a physical disability or illness has no direct effect on intellectual growth or development." (Hunt & Marshall, 1994, p. 448). Teachers must be aware of this relationship and cognizant of possible bias concerning the cognitive development of students with physical disabilities. Fortunately, technological advances (such as specialized computer equipment) have rapidly improved the opportunity for classroom communication.

The literature selections feature children with many types of physical disabilities. Through these literature selections, children can vicariously experience the challenges and accomplishments of the those with physical disabilities. They become aware of services, equipment, therapy, and personnel that aid in the inclusion of these individuals.

REFERENCES

Hunt, N., & Marshall, K. (1994). *Exceptional children and youth*. Boston: Houghton Mifflin Company.

Lewis, R. B., & Doorlag, D. H. (1987). Teaching special students in the mainstream. (2nd ed.). Columbus, OH: Merrill Publishers.

U.S. Department of Education. (1997). Nineteenth annual report to Congress on the implementation of the Individuals with Disabilities Education Act. Washington, DC: U.S. Government Printing Office.

LITERATURE SELECTIONS

 Aiello, B. & Shulman, J. (1988). *It's Your Turn at Bat*. Frederick, MD: Twenty-first Century Books.

Mark is a boy who has cerebral palsy and uses a wheelchair. He also has difficulty speaking, especially when he gets upset. The book depicts one part of Mark's life. He is shown playing baseball and managing his team. Questions that children frequently ask and Mark's responses are at the end of the book. This comfortable interchange provides helpful and interesting information that may serve to remove some of the mystery about disabilities.

 • Research information on different kinds of wheelchairs to share with the students. Call a hospital equipment rental business and ask them to demonstrate different types of wheelchairs.

• Mark and Brenda become friends. Write a diamante poem about them. (See format in Appendix A.)

- Write your own mini-biography or biographical sketch using "Meet Mark" as a sample.

- Sit in a chair and try to bat a ball.

- Mark's writing topic was "The Sewing Machine: How It Changes Our Lives." Identify something that you think has had a great effect on the way we live. Investigate and write about it.

- Both Brenda and Mark enjoyed learning about something that they found uninteresting at first. Make a list of three things that don't interest you and learn two things about each.

- Write about your favorite hero.

- Mark calls his wheelchair his Cruiser. Do you have an unusual name for something you use?

- If you could ask Mark another question about cerebral palsy, what would it be?

- Mark has a special ball and a bigger bat to help him play baseball. Design other sports equipment that might help those with disabilities.

- Write about a dream that you have had that, like Mark, made you scared to fall back asleep.

 Berenstein, S., & Berenstein, J. (1993). *Berenstein Bears and the Wheelchair Commando*. New York: Random House.

This is the story of Harry, who has just moved into the neighborhood. Harry was injured in a car accident and is now in a wheelchair. At the start of the story he is bitter about his condition, and feels that all the other "cubs" are not interested in befriending him because of his disability. He eventually makes friends with some of his classmates; however, four boys continue to tease him. The climax occurs when one of these boys challenges him to a game of basketball. Insisting that the boy also play in a wheelchair, Harry agrees to the challenge and wins. He gains the respect of all the students.

- Invite a computer expert to demonstrate helpful software for students with disabilities.

- Mrs. McGill says that it isn't healthy for Harry to have only other children with disabilities for friends. Do you think that is true?

- Harry has a ramp in front of his house to help him get in and out in his wheelchair. What are some buildings you are familiar with that have ramps or other wheelchair facilities?

- Why do you think Harry is unfriendly when he first goes to school?

- Make an "I can do" book. Share your books with the class.

- The book begins with a description of the bears' neighborhood and school friends. Make a list of children from your neighborhood who go to school with you. Write three words to describe each child.

- Harry spends a lot of time on his computer after school. Make a list of the things you do after school. Tally the number of minutes you spend on each activity and display it in a bar graph.

- Queenie made Harry feel welcome at school. Say something to someone at school to make him or her feel special.

- Why didn't Harry raise his hand as a computer expert?

- Harry felt left out at school. Tell or write about a time that you felt that way.

- Mr. McGill asked Harry about his teacher. Write a short note to your parents telling them about your teacher.

- Make a list of things that you do well and things you would like to improve.

- Brother becomes a hero. Write a cinquain about someone you regard as a hero. (See format in appendix A.)

 Bergman, T. (1989). *On Our Own Terms: Children Living with Physical Disabilities.* Milwaukee: Gareth Stevens.

> This book introduces the reader to several children with various physical disabilities who come to the Karolinska Hospital in Stockholm, Sweden, a clinic for these types of conditions. The sensitive black and white photographs depict the therapy and hard work these children must endure. Together with the text, these photographs make children more aware of treatments for children with physical disabilities.

 - Invite a physical or occupational therapist to come to class and share information about his or her career.

• See "Things to Do and Think About" in the back of the book.

 • In the back of the book are some addresses of places to write for more information on physical disabilities. With your class, compose a letter to one of these places.

• Create an invention that might help one of the children in this book.

• Each of the children in this book must work hard to achieve small successes. Make a book, *The Story of My Success*, where you draw and write about one of your successes.

• Work with the physical education teacher to try rolling on a roller as Kicki does or on a scooter as Helena does.

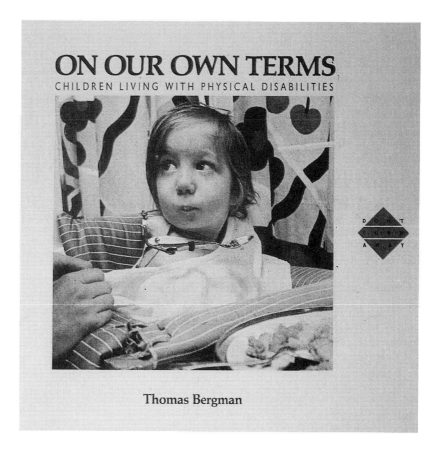

Figure 2-1 *On Our Own Terms: Children Living with Physical Disabilities* by T. Bergman (1989). Cover reprinted with permission of Gareth Stevens.

- Select one of the children portrayed in the book. Pretend that he or she is your friend. Write about the things you do together.

- Discuss the questions and answers on pages 42–44 in the book.

 Carlson, N. (1990). *Arnie and the New Kid.* **New York: Viking.**

The characters in this book are portrayed by animals. Philip is a new boy at school with a physical disability (he is in a wheelchair). Arnie teases Philip about his disability until he falls, sustains some injuries, and discovers what it is like to have a disability. Arnie and Philip become friends and Arnie refers to Philip as his "coach."

- Initiate a discussion about teasing, how it hurts people, etc.

- In the story, Arnie had to eat peas with his left hand, which was hard for him. Try using the hand that you don't write with to eat lunch. Be ready to report on what happened.

- Arnie and Philip find many things to do together. Pretend you are the illustrator of the book and draw some other ways they might have fun together.

- How could you help someone in a wheelchair get around better at school?

- Tell about a time when you were teased. How did you handle it?

- Have you ever been new to the class or school? How did you make friends?

- What computer games do you enjoy playing with a friend?

 Caseley, J. (1991). *Harry and Willy and Carrothead.* **New York: Greenwillow Books.**

Harry was born without a left hand and was fitted with a prosthesis when he was four years old. The children at school are very curious about his arm. One child, Oscar (called Carrothead because of his red hair), becomes Harry's good friend. When another boy, Willy, teases Oscar because of his hair, Harry defends his friend. Harry and Willy and Oscar become best friends, accepting each other's "disabilities."

• Harry wears a prosthesis. Invite a bioengineer or someone who wears a prosthesis to class to talk about and demonstrate it.

• Has anyone called you something that you didn't like? What did you do?

• Harry, Willy, and Oscar became good friends. Write a story about something you enjoy doing with your friends.

• Gather information about the development of prostheses. How is technology contributing to their effectiveness?

• Why did the children gather around Harry when they first met him at school?

• Do you think Oscar liked to be called Carrothead? Why or why not?

• In what ways did the prosthesis help Harry in the story? How else might a prosthesis help someone in daily life?

• Like Oscar, write a story about you and your friends. Illustrate your story.

 Damrell, L. (1991). *With the Wind*. New York: Orchard Books.

This is a story about the delight a young boy feels as he rides a horse. Written in poetic style with vivid illustrations to match, the reader experiences the strength and sense of power that comes with the ride. It is not until the end of the book as the boy dismounts from the horse that his leg braces and waiting wheelchair are visible. The reality is in sharp contrast to the freedom he imagined while on the horse.

 • Invite an orthopedic specialist to class to discuss leg injuries and various apparatus.

 • Take a field trip to a riding stable to learn more about horses and perhaps do some beginning riding.

• Did the ending surprise you? Why?

• Do you think that the boy was really strengthened by riding the horse? Why?

• Gather information about different kinds of horses. Make a graph showing their average height, weight, speed, and anything else that you find interesting.

- The boy feels a sense of power and freedom when he rides. Write about something that makes you feel that way.

- How do you think the horses help the boy feel?

- Close your eyes and picture what else the boy might see on his ride. Draw a picture of what you imagine.

- Write a poem or an acrostic about "freedom." (See format in Appendix A.)

 Emmert, M. (1989). *I'm the Big Sister Now.* Morton Grove, IL: Albert Whitman.

This is a true story about two sisters, Michelle and Amy Emmert. Amy was born severely disabled with cerebral palsy. Michelle, Amy's younger sister, describes the joys and difficulties they experienced together as children. It is a lovingly told story. A discussion about cerebral palsy, written by Eugene E. Bleck, M.D., is on the last page.

- Initiate a discussion about special people in our lives—sisters, brothers, friends, etc.

- Write to the National Cerebral Palsy Foundation for information about cerebral palsy and the most recent research about its diagnosis and treatment.

- Read about the people who are extra special to Amy. Write about the people who are special to you.

- Amy has a special gift that she gives to people. What is it?

- What are some other ways that Michelle might help her big sister Amy?

- In the story, the author says that Amy likes birthday parties. What are some presents you could give her that she might like?

- There are many scrapbook pictures of Amy and her family in the book. Bring a picture of your family that shows how you help each other. Be ready to tell about it.

 Fassler, J. (1975). *Howie Helps Himself.* Morton Grove, IL: Albert Whitman.

Howie is a little boy who is in a wheelchair due to a physical disability. The reader experiences the range of emotions and reactions of this picture book

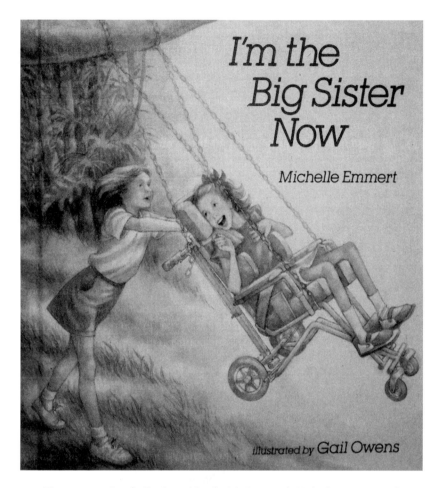

Figure 2-2   *I'm the Big Sister Now* by M. Emmert (1989). Cover reprinted
by permission of Albert Whitman.

character as he strives to achieve his one special wish: to move his wheelchair
by himself. After much struggle and practice, Howie manages to reach his
goal when he pushes his wheelchair to meet his father. Howie and his father
delight in his accomplishment.

 • Ask a bus driver to demonstrate the elevator lift on a bus.

• Ask women with disabilities to speak to the class (in this and many other
books, the main character is male).

• Describe a time when there was something that you really wanted to do
but didn't know how to. How did you feel? How do you think Howie feels?

- When Howie pushed his wheelchair, his dad hugged him but didn't say anything. What do you think he was thinking? With a partner, write a dialogue and be prepared to act it out.

- If Howie went to your school, could he move easily around the classroom? The school?

- Draw a self-portrait and describe yourself in words under the picture.

- Visit a museum that offers the opportunity to experience using a wheelchair.

- Howie enjoys going to the park with his grandmother. Write about something you enjoy doing with a special person.

- Howie had to practice moving his wheelchair. Tell about a time when you had to practice something.

 Hearn, E. (1984). *Good Morning, Franny, Good Night, Franny.* Toronto, Canada: Women's Press.

Franny is a little girl in a wheelchair, who is happy because she can now move around easily outside since it is spring. Franny soon meets Ting and the two become good friends, greeting each other and saying "good night" every evening. After Franny is released from a visit to the hospital, she discovers that Ting has moved away. However, she left her messages, "Good morning, Franny" and "Good night, Franny" painted in the sidewalk, where it stayed even after the snow.

- Demonstrate how to divide a paper into four squares and draw four pictures that tell the main ideas of the story.

- Franny and Ting are special to each other. Talk about the things they do for each other.

- Tell about special friends you have. What do you enjoy doing together?

- Write a message to a special friend. Display these on a "Messages" bulletin board.

- Franny was upset when Ting moved away. Have you ever had to move or has a good friend moved away? How did you feel?

- Draw or write a picture on the pavement using sidewalk chalk.

Kehret, P. (1996). *Small Steps: The Year I Got Polio.* **Morton Grove, IL: Albert Whitman.**

This is the author's true story of her diagnosis and experience with polio at the age of twelve. Through powerful treatments and physical therapy, she keeps a positive outlook. With the love and support of her family and her strong determination she progresses to the point of using "walking sticks." After seven months, she returns to school, in many ways stronger than when she left.

 • Sheltering Arms Hospital was the rehabilitation center where Peg spent her time. Invite a rehabilitation therapist to tell about his or her job.

 • Discuss President Roosevelt and his polio story.

• Polio used to be an epidemic, but is now almost nonexistent thanks to vaccines. Find out about these vaccines and what they do.

• The author dreamed of being a writer from the time she was young. What do you dream of doing?

• Read *The Velveteen Rabbit* and talk about this story in relation to the book.

• The author's story is a little like a diary of events. Keep a diary of your own, or start a dialogue journal to communicate with your teacher.

 Krementz, J. (1992). *How It Feels to Live with a Physical Disability.* **New York: Simon & Schuster.**

The book features stories about twelve children with physical disabilities including paralysis, cerebral palsy, and dwarfism. Each portrayal is a heart-warming account of the daily trials and accomplishments of the children. They tell their own stories, which are accompanied by photographs that both inform and inspire the reader.

 • Lead the class in a discussion about a new invention that could help a person with a physical disability (maybe one of the people in this book). Encourage students to draw this invention.

• The first boy, Eli, says that his mom is a wonderful listener. Who is a good listener in your life? Why is it important to be a good listener?

• Write a story about a boy or girl who thought they couldn't do something, but later found out that they could. Like Ivonne, they never gave up.

- Katherine's dad said, "If you carry out what you believe in, you'll always reach your goal." What does that mean to you?

- How are the people in this book all alike?

- Explore the lives of dwarfs or midgets, such as the people who played parts in the "The Wizard of Oz." What special difficulties might a small person experience?

- Write to one of the foundations to gather more information about one of the conditions/syndromes.

- Write to one of the national sports organizations for information about activities and events for the disabled.

 Lasker, J. (1980). *Nick Joins In*. Morton Grove, IL: Albert Whitman.

Nick, who is in a wheelchair, is getting ready to enter a new school that has become wheelchair accessible. He is apprehensive about what the other children will say. However, his fears are quickly put to rest as the children welcome him. Nick makes some new friends but gains everyone's attention when he is able to retrieve a ball which is caught in the gutter of the school.

 • Lead the class in a walk around the school building. Discuss: Is the school prepared for a student in a wheelchair? What problems might he or she encounter?

- If you were a student in Nick's class, what would you like to ask him?

- What else could the teacher and students do to welcome Nick?

- Even though Nick cannot run and jump, he helps his classmates by getting the ball down from the roof. Write about a time when you did something special for someone.

- Nick was worried about going to school. He asked a lot of questions about what it would be like. Think about some of the things you worry about before the start of a new school year. Create a brochure or poster advertising your class that may help someone new feel comfortable.

- Nick's new classmates were given an opportunity to ask him questions. Make a list of questions that you think Nick would have liked to ask them.

Meyer, G., & Meyer, M. (1992). A *Very Special Critter*. Racine, WI: Western Publishing Company.

The new critter at school, Alex, is in a wheelchair. While everyone thought that he needed a lot of help at first, they soon discovered that he was capable of doing many things himself and enjoyed doing the same things they did. Sometimes Alex did the helping.

 • Have students work in cooperative groups and brainstorm ways to make a new student feel comfortable.

 • Prepare a welcome bag or folder for a new student. Include the names of everyone in the class, a list of school rules, a schedule, a welcome note, perhaps some stickers or a small treat and anything else that seems appropriate.

• Write a welcome note to a new student or to a classmate that you don't talk with very often.

• Alex is able to do many things with his wheelchair. Draw a wheelchair of the future. What would it be able to do? Could it have a small cooler attached for drinks? Could a television or video games be attached?

 Muldoon, K. M. (1989). *Princess Pooh*. Morton Grove, IL: Albert Whitman.

Patty Jean Pipers secretly refers to her big sister Penelope as Princess Pooh. Patty thinks that her sister has quite the life as she sits on her "throne" and gets lots of attention. When Patty takes the "throne" she learns that being confined to a wheelchair is not as easy or as much fun as she thought it was. She discovers that she has been wrong, that her parents really do care about her, and that she should just enjoy being Penelope's sister.

 • Arrange for the class to try out a wheelchair on various surfaces. Some hands-on museums offer this experience. Or have someone from a home health care facility bring in a wheelchair for the children to try.

• Patty secretly refers to her sister Penelope as Princess Pooh. Do you have nicknames or secret names for anyone in your family or friends?

• Patty thinks that she is treated unfairly. Write a letter to someone you feel has treated you unfairly. Describe the situation and explain how you feel.

- Patty describes the chores that each member of her family is responsible for. Make a Venn diagram showing the responsibility distribution in your family.

- People looked at Patty and then turned away. Some boys teased her. Write a journal entry about how you think Patty felt.

- Patty realizes that her parents really do care about her. Make a list of ways that your parents or others who are important to you show that they care about you. Write that person a thank-you letter.

- At the end of the story Patty decides that it is nice to be Penelope's sister. Continue the story. Write about what happens in the next few days.

 Rabe, B. (1981). *The Balancing Girl*. New York: E. P. Dutton.

Margaret is a first grader whose disability requires her to wear braces and use crutches or a wheelchair, and whose special talent is balancing all kinds of things. In her effort to impress Tommy, she comes up with a terrific balancing idea for the school carnival. Her domino event is the most successful in the carnival.

 • Look in the *Guinness Book of World Records* for the greatest numbers of dominoes set up. Share this and other facts from the book with your class.

- (before reading) Margaret is the name of the girl in this story who is good at balancing. What do you think she might balance?

- Try some balancing activities that Margaret did and some of your own.

- Set up a domino pattern and knock it down or ask a friend to do it.

- Write about or draw an idea that you have for a carnival booth.

- Even though Margaret has a disability, she uses her special balancing talent to help earn money at the school carnival. Draw a picture of yourself performing a special talent that you have.

- Retell the story so that Tommy is nice to Margaret.

- Find one nice thing to say to someone each day of the week. Write down what you say and how the person responds.

- Why do you think Tommy reacted the way he did?

Raffi. (1988). *One Light, One Sun*. New York: Crown Publishers.

This warmly illustrated Raffi song shows the sun rising, shining, and setting on three diverse families who live next door to each other. Throughout one day, the reader views their various activities at home and in the neighborhood. One family includes a child in a wheelchair.

- Sing the song at the end of the book with your class. Students could add gestures or dance.

- Write a story—One Night, One Moon—modeling this story.

- Draw a picture of the inside of your home in the morning or at night.

- What is the main idea of this story?

- Select a page and write a story about what is happening in the home.

- Draw a picture of your neighborhood. Make a list of all the ways you and your neighbors are alike.

- Make a diorama of one scene in the book.

 Roy, R. (1985). *Move Over, Wheelchairs Coming Through*. New York: Clarion Books.

Seven young people talk about their lives. The disabilities presented include arthrogryposis, hemolymphangioma, cerebral palsy, spina bifida, and muscular dystrophy. In addition to the candid information about the daily experiences of these people, information from nurses, doctors, therapists, psychologists, and hospital aides assist the reader in understanding the implications of the physical disabilities.

- Invite a specialist to demonstrate different types of wheelchairs to the class.

- Many of these children see a physical therapist. Invite a physical therapist to class to explain his or her job.

- The book describes some laws that have helped people with disabilities. Do research on some other important laws that affect people with disabilities.

- Lizzy can't go to some classes because they are on the second floor. Is your school wheelchair accessible?

- Walk around your school. Make a list of things that could help or hinder someone in a wheelchair.

- Sometimes people stare at people with disabilities because they are scared or don't understand. What should you do?

- Wear a headband with a long wooden pointer similar to what Scott has in the photograph. Sit at the classroom computer. Try to type a short message to a friend.

- Write to the Muscular Dystrophy Association to get more information on that disease.

- Make a list of all the special devices that the children in the book used.

- Check the local YMCA/YWCA to see if they offer adaptive swimming classes.

 Russo, M. (1992). *Alex Is My Friend.* **New York: Greenwillow Books.**

This is a story of the friendship shared by two little boys. Ben talks about all the things they enjoy doing together, as well as his friend's disability. Alex needed back surgery and used a wheelchair. He will always be small and not able to do some things as well as other children. Ben's narration and the wonderful illustrations take the reader through all of their experiences.

 • Invite an orthopedic surgeon to talk about Alex's condition.

- Write an acrostic poem about friends. (See format in appendix A.)

- Alex and Ben have been friends since they were little. Do you have any friends you have had since you were little? How did you meet?

- What are some other gifts that Ben could have brought for Alex to play with in bed?

- Alex knows a lot of jokes. Tell a joke that you know.

- Is Ben a good friend to Alex? How can you tell?

- The book begins with the telling of how the two boys met and became friends. Write and illustrate a story about how you met one of your friends.

- Alex's friend Ben brought Alex a present after his surgery. Make cards for children who are in the hospital pediatric care unit.

- Draw or write about a present that you would take to your friend if he or she were in the hospital or ill.

- Design a book that tells about all the things that you enjoy doing with one of your friends.

 Seuling, B. (1986). *I'm Not So Different.* **New York: Golden.**

The book features Kit who is in a wheelchair. Written in the first person, Kit describes her life at home and at school. The main event centers around Kit's excursion to a concert with her father and her friend to hear her favorite group play. When her friend manages to get through the crowd without her to get an autograph, Kit feels as though she is different from others because of her disability. However, when the leader of the band speaks directly to her as he leaves, Kit is delighted and says that maybe she isn't so different after all.

- Ask a bus driver to show the class the elevator for wheelchairs on the bus.

- Investigate places in the community that offer special activities for children or adults with disabilities. Arrange for a field trip to one of these places.

- Kit has nicknames that other people call her. Do you have any nicknames or do you wish you had one?

- Kit has chores to do in her house. What jobs are you responsible for? Do a survey and gather information about the kinds of jobs your classmates do. Display your findings in a graph.

- Kit's dad said, "Everyone is different from everyone else." What did he mean by that?

 Smith, E. S. (1988). *A Service Dog Goes to School*. New York: Morrow Junior Books.

This book describes how service dogs learn to perform their tasks, which bring independence to people whose movement is limited. Licorice is one such dog who was chosen as a puppy for this work, trained extensively, and eventually became the arms and hands of Scott, a wheelchair-bound boy. Licorice proves that she is the best friend ever when she successfully accompanies Scott to school, helps him through the day, and makes it possible for him to play with his friends.

- Write to Canine Companions for Independence, P.O. Box 446, Santa Rosa, California 95402-0446 for information on puppy raising for service dogs. Share this information with the class.

- Invite a community person who uses a service dog to come and talk to the class.

- Fold a paper into four squares. Draw four things that service dogs must learn to do.

- If you have a pet, tell about the ways you have trained the pet.

- What types of pets can be trained?

 Tylor, R. (1991). *All By Self*. Boulder, CO: Light On Books.

All By Self is a father's story about his young son, who, at a very young age, was struck with an illness that left him with cerebral palsy. Written in a simple poetic style, it tells of the boy's challenges and triumphs. Included in the back of the book is an expanded adult version, which is, like the text, very inspiring.

- Invite a nurse or health care professional to tell more about cerebral palsy.

- Mical is included in a regular classroom. If Mical were in your class, what could you do to help him?

- Mical and his father have a special relationship. Tell about someone who is special to you.

- Mical's first words were "Light on." Find out what your first words were and share them with the class.

- Dad and Mical enjoy the beach together. Tell about a special place you like to visit. Draw a picture of this place.

 Wanous, S. (1995). *Sara's Secret*. Minneapolis: Carolrhoda Books.

Sara is a new girl at school. Her five-year-old brother, Justin, has cerebral palsy, is mentally retarded, and attends the special education class at the same school. Sara, however, keeps this a secret. When Sara's class studies about disabilities, the teacher asks the students to bring in something that could help a person with a disability. Caught between her love for her brother and her fear of her classmates' responses, Sara must decide whether to risk sharing her secret with the class. She brings Justin to class and the children are very receptive.

- Invite a pediatrician to class to explain more about cerebral palsy.

- Make a list of people who could help a person with cerebral palsy. For example, a person called a "physical therapist" could help with muscular stiffness.

- Sara has a special secret. Do you have any secrets? Why do you think Sara decided to share her secret?

- Sara says that her brother "teaches us how to understand each other better." Write what you think she means by that.

- Have a show-and-tell day in your class.

 Wells, R. (1990). *The Little Lame Prince.* **New York: Dial Books for Young Readers.**

Rosemary Wells retells a favorite story from her own childhood, *The Little Lame Prince* by Dinah Maria Mulock Craik. By the time Prince Francisco is three years old, he is disabled, his parents are dead, and his wicked uncle has seized the throne and exiled the prince to a desolate land. Francisco grows up not knowing that he is a prince. With a magical gift from his fairy godmother, he returns to his kingdom and lives happily ever after.

- Lead the class in a discussion of how the story might be different if Francisco knew he was a prince.

- If you had a fairy godmother like Francisco, what would you wish for?

- How do you know that Franciso had a "wise head and kind heart"?

- Write about and illustrate an adventure you would have if you had a magic cape.

- Write a poem that summarizes the story.

 Whinston, J. L. (1989). *I'm Joshua and "Yes I Can."* **New York: Vantage Press.**

Joshua, a boy with cerebral palsy, is about to begin first grade in a regular classroom. The reader follows his story as he gets up in the morning, does his morning exercises, eats breakfast, and goes to school. During all this time, he has many doubts and worries about what will happen when he gets there. Reassured by his parents and brother and sister, he gains the confidence to go and repeats to himself, "Yes, I can." Joshua finds out that everyone has things they can't do.

- Invite a physical therapist or occupational therapist in to discuss ways to help those with cerebral palsy.

- Draw a picture of yourself doing something you do well. Display these on a "Yes, I Can!" bulletin board.

- How do you think Joshua felt when he fell and all the children were laughing and pointing at him? What should they have done in that situation?

- One girl says that she felt a little scared when Joshua fell. Why would she feel scared?

- Joshua was chosen for the school choir. What school activities are you involved in or would you like to be involved in?

 White, P. (1978). *Janet at School*. New York: Thomas Y. Crowell Company.

Janet is a five-year-old girl with spina bifida. She attends a neighborhood school with her friends. Although she can't do everything the others do because she uses a wheelchair, she finds her own ways to participate. Colorful photographs show Janet twirling the jump rope for her friends and camping with her family. This book helps young readers understand spina bifida and realize that those with this disability are not limited in many respects.

- Guide the class in doing further research on spina bifida. Is there more than one type of spina bifida? What types of equipment can help those with spina bifida?

- Try using a piece of gym or playground equipment with just your arms. What are some problems that you think Janet has?

- Janet's family likes to go camping. What does your family do for fun? Bring in some pictures to show the class.

 Wolf, B. (1974). *Don't Feel Sorry for Paul*. Philadelphia: J. B. Lippincott.

Paul is a six-year-old boy who wears a prosthesis for his right arm and one for each of his legs. With these aids, Paul plays, works, and even rides horses competitively. In spite of these accomplishments, there are some people who feel sorry for him and others who laugh at him. The text and sensitive photos capture Paul's reactions and many experiences in two weeks of his life.

- Invite a bioengineer in to demonstrate how a prosthesis works.

- Visit a riding stable. Have someone demonstrate the care of a horse and the English style of riding. Arrange for an initial riding lesson if possible.

- The author describes how Paul gets ready for school in the morning. Make a list of what you do in the morning to get dressed and ready for school.

- Paul has a difficult time with his right leg prosthesis. Talk, write about, or draw something that was difficult for you to do. How did you master it? Who helped you?

- Sunday is Paul's favorite day of the week. What is your favorite day? What do you enjoy doing on that day?

- Paul and his family enjoy an Italian dinner together. Make a menu for a dinner that you think your family would enjoy.

- The story describes Paul's birthday party. Write about or draw your favorite birthday or plan a birthday celebration for someone in your family.

- Paul received lots of presents for his birthday. Draw a picture or write about a present that you would like to give someone special.

- Why does Paul's mother feel that he doesn't need anyone to feel sorry for him?

 Yates. S. (1992). *Can't You Be Still?* Winnipeg, Manitoba, Canada: Gemma B. Publishing, Inc.

Ann, a four-year-old girl with cerebral palsy, is going to a new school. As she tries to adjust, she knocks a boy's glasses off with her "wild right," her arm that "moves without waiting for a signal." The teacher explains a little about cerebral palsy, but the real lesson comes when the children see how well Ann can swim.

- Invite a physician to instruct the children about cerebral palsy.

- Ann has a special ability to swim. What types of activities do you do well?

- Jay is a special friend to Ann. Tell or write about your special friend.

- If Ann were in your class, what could you do to help her?

CHAPTER 3

LITERATURE ABOUT CHILDREN WITH HEARING IMPAIRMENTS

The Individuals with Disabilities Education Act (IDEA) mandates service for children who are deaf and hard of hearing. Although both groups have difficulty processing linguistic information, those who are hard of hearing can usually understand oral speech with the use of hearing aids. Deafness precludes this ability. About thirty percent of children with a hearing impairment also have other disabilities.

According to the Nineteenth Annual Report to Congress on the Implementation of the Individuals with Disabilities Education Act (1997), approximately 68,070 children between the ages of six and twenty-one are identified as having a hearing loss—one percent of the total number of children with disabilities.

Language is a critical area affected by hearing loss. Most children who are deaf or hard of hearing come to school with a language delay. Classroom implications are vast. First, young children may have a unique "first language"—sometimes an invented combination of language and gestures that only the family understands (Luetke-Stahlman & Luckner, 1991). Acquisition of the English language may not begin until after they enter school, and tends to be much slower than that of hearing children (Paul & Jackson, 1993). Second, limited use of language is often mistakenly associated with cognitive impairment. Recent research concludes that people who are deaf and hard of hearing as a group have normal cognitive and intellectual abilities. Their average school achievement, however, is below that of their peers who hear (Paul & Jackson, 1993), largely due to a lag in reading performance that hinges on mastery of the English language.

Children who are deaf tend to have more adjustment problems than children who hear (Meadow-Orlans, 1980). These largely arise from experiences within the family, school, or community due to lack of communication.

35

Many children who are hearing impaired use assistive listening devices (hearing aids, FM systems) to facilitate communication and promote academic achievement. Occasionally, oral or sign language interpreters accompany a child to the general education classroom.

One controversial issue concerns whether to use sign language. Some believe that the use of oral communication permits people with hearing loss to function in the hearing world. A concern is that individuals using sign language never become fluent speakers. Others advocate signing as an exclusive mode of communication. Still other experts contend that a combination of lip-reading, speech, and signing provides "total" communication for people who are hearing-impaired (Rudman, 1995). Teachers should be aware of the child's preferred mode of communication, be it oral, sign language, or a combination, and communicate with the child using the appropriate system.

The literature selections depict children of various age levels with hearing loss. Incidental factual information about hearing loss is integrated into some of the selections. Readers encounter children using a variety of available aids. Teachers could use several of the selections to facilitate sign language instruction and to develop understanding of communication both inside and outside the hearing-impaired/deaf community.

REFERENCES

Luetke-Stahlman, B., & Luckner, J. (1991). *Effectively educating students with hearing impairments*. New York: Longman.

Meadow-Orlans, K. P. (1980). *Deafness and child development*. Berkeley: University of California Press.

Paul, P. V., & Jackson, D. W. (1993). *Toward a psychology of deafness*. Boston: Allyn & Bacon.

Rudman, M. K. (1995). *Children's literature: An issues approach*. New York: Longman.

U.S. Department of Education. (1997). Nineteenth annual report to Congress on the implementation of the Individuals with Disabilities Education Act. Washington, DC: U.S. Government Printing Office.

LITERATURE SELECTION

 Abramson, M. (1985). *Amy, the Story of a Deaf Child*. New York: Lodestar Books.

Amy is a remarkable fifth-grade girl who is deaf. She has a brother who hears and parents who are also deaf. Amy goes to school with friends who hear; she is the only person in her school who is deaf. The story details the assistance

Amy receives through her hearing aid, interpreters, and communication systems. The reader comes to understand that Amy, like all children who are deaf, likes to do many of the same things that children who hear like to do, but that she must do some things differently.

 • Amy talks about her favorite authors and books. Do a class survey to determine favorite authors. Display the information in a bar graph.

 • Amy uses a TTY—a teletypewriter-telephone. Invite someone from a telephone company to demonstrate the device.

- Amy's brother, John, is a special person in her life because he defends her when other children make fun of her. Tell about someone in your life like John.

- Make a list of the good things and the difficult things about being deaf.

- Practice lip reading with a friend. Describe your experience. Was it easy or difficult?

- Amy is thinking about what she wants to be when she grows up. Draw a picture of yourself in your chosen career.

- What difficulties might Amy's family encounter since both her parents are deaf?

- Amy talks about her mom fixing her hair and helping her with homework. Make a list of things your mom or another special person helps you with. Select some of your ideas and create a cinquain poem about you and your mom or other special person. (See format in Appendix A.)

- Amy describes her dad as "cute" and a "softie." Write a list of words that describe your dad. Turn them into a poem.

- Practice some of the signs that Amy demonstrates in the back of the book. Teach them to a friend.

- Amy and Carolyn play hide-and seek two different ways. Think of another way to play one of the games that you enjoy playing with friends.

- Amy's favorite things at recess are the swings and the obstacle course. Draw your favorite playground activity. Draw or write about something you wish you could do during recess.

- Amy has an interpreter with her at school. Where have you seen an interpreter?

- Amy usually tries to do her homework right after school and then she reads. For one week, make a chart of the things you do after school.

- Write to one of the organizations listed in the back of the book for more information about your area of interest.

 Aseltine, L., Mueller, E., & Tait, N. (1986). *I'm Deaf and It's Okay*. Morton Grove IL: Albert Whitman.

The young boy in this story describes his frustrations with being deaf and having to wear hearing aids. He hopes that when he grows up, he'll no longer have to wear them. When a teenager who is also deaf encourages him by telling him that he can do what people who hear can do, he thinks that maybe it will be okay to be grown up and wear hearing aids.

 • Invite an audiologist or hearing aid specialist to demonstrate how hearing aids work.

- Try some of the signs in the back of the book. Teach them to a friend.

- Why do you think the boy in this story feels the way he does?

- What could his friends do to help him?

- Make a list of the things you learned from the book about talking to people who are deaf.

- Brian is a special friend to the boy. Tell about a special friend that you have.

- The boy and his teacher use an FM system to help him hear in the classroom. Find out more about aids to help people hear.

 Bergman, T. (1989). *Finding a Common Language: Children Living with Deafness*. Milwaukee: Gareth Stevens.

Lina, a six-year-old girl who is almost completely deaf, is depicted in this book. Both the text and remarkable pictures portray her life at home and at her preschool for the deaf. She has many challenges and frustrations throughout the days, and the reader sees how she copes with these. Lina, like any child, has hopes, joys, and sorrows; her disability does not make her different.

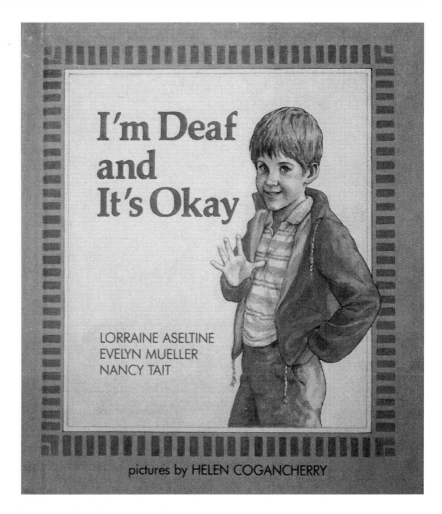

Figure 3-1 *I'm Deaf and It's Okay* by L. Aseltine, E. Mueller, & N. Tait (1986). Cover reprinted by permission of Albert Whitman.

 • Invite someone to come and explain how adaptive aquatics works.

 • Invite someone to speak about types of adaptive equipment for those who are deaf.

 • See "Things to Do and Talk About" on pages 45–46.

• Lina has to have a hearing aid. Talk about a time when you had a hearing test.

• Discuss what is meant by the term "universal language."

Figure 3-2 *Finding a Common Language* by T. Bergman (1989).
Cover reprinted by permission of Gareth Stevens.

- In the back of the book are many questions about deafness. What questions do you have?

- Choose a song and dance to it, moving with the beat.

 Booth, B. D. (1991). *Mandy*. New York: Lothrop, Lee & Shepard Books.

Mandy and Grandma live together in the country and have a very special relationship. They are shown baking cookies, dancing, perusing a photo album, and going for a walk. Mandy becomes a heroine when she returns to the woods during a storm to find her Grandma's treasured silver pin that was lost. Beautiful paintings illustrate this warmly told story about a very special child who is deaf.

- Bake cookies together as a class and then enjoy them with milk.

- What sounds would you miss most if you couldn't hear?

- Mandy's grandmother is very special to her. Tell about a special person in your life.

- Mandy and Grandma enjoy dancing together. Turn on some music and move to it—individually or with partners.

- Mandy's grandmother's pin is a special keepsake. Write about or draw one of your special treasures.

- Choose a sound that is familiar to you. Write a description of that sound for Mandy.

- Mandy describes a time at camp when she was very frightened. Tell about a time you were frightened and what you did about it.

- Do Mandy and her grandmother need a lot of words to communicate? Why?

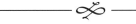

 Charlip, R., Beth, M., & Ancona, G. (1974). *Handtalk: An ABC of Finger Spelling and Sign Language.* **New York: Four Winds Press.**

This picture book communicates in full-color photographs two different languages—finger spelling and sign language. For each letter of the alphabet, there is a word that is being signed by a person in the photograph as well as finger spelled using small pictures at the bottom of the page. Children learn many of the signs and positions for finger spelling since they are encouraged to decode the words on their own.

- Research other ways that the deaf might communicate. Discuss these with the class.

- Make up a secret code with a friend. Practice communicating with each other.

- Learn some of the signs in the book. Teach them to a friend or family member.

- People who communicate for those who are deaf are called interpreters. Where have you seen an interpreter at work?

- Try to compose a sentence using sign language.

- With a partner or in a small group, make up new signs or expressions for words or ideas. Try to communicate with each other. Then try to teach the signs to someone else.

- Practice "The Very Ugly Village" (a poem depicted through sign at the end of the book). Do the poem together in a small group or in unison with the whole class.

 Greenberg, J. E. (1985). *What Is the Sign for Friend?* New York: Franklin Watts.

Shane likes pizza, soccer, swimming, and playing just like other boys his age. However, Shane is almost completely deaf and wears a hearing aid. The story and pictures in this book detail the experiences of Shane at home, with his friends, and in his classroom with children who hear. Signs for special words are included throughout the book for the reader.

 • Read the *Sesame Street Sign Language* book to your class.

 • Shane works with a speech therapist who helps him improve his speech. Invite a speech therapist in to talk about the things he or she does.

 • In the book, Ms. Smith helps Shane improve his speech through speech therapy. Discuss the connection between hearing and the ability to speak clearly.

 • Invite a representative from a television station to explain how closed captioning devices work for individuals with hearing loss.

- Shane enjoys having a special treat with his family—sometimes pizza. What is your favorite treat to share with your family?

- Learn to make the signs that are illustrated in the book.

- Shane and Mitchell enjoy playing on a soccer team. Write a story or draw a picture of something you especially enjoy doing with a friend.

- Shane's dad wakes him up in the morning. Who wakes you up? Write a short story about a typical school morning.

- Shane has an interpreter in his classroom. Where else might you see an interpreter at work?

- Practice the sign language that is shown in the book. Teach a friend or brother or sister this language.

- Make up a story for a book using only the pictures. Compare it to the real story. Think about how Shane and others like him may miss out on details of stories and television programs.

 Hodges, C. (1995). *When I Grow Up*. Hollidaysburg, PA: Jason and Nordic Publishers.

Over milk and cookies, Jimmy's mom explains that he will always wear hearing aids. To help him understand growing up, they participate in a Career Day bus trip. They visit a zookeeper, art teacher, lawn care business owner, waiter, boat builder, computer programmer, and a paper boy who are all deaf. Jimmy decides that when he grows up, he will be deaf and anything else he wants to be. Numerous signs for words are illustrated throughout the book and in a dictionary at the end of the book.

- Help students learn some of the signs presented in the book. Invite someone who signs to help.

- Jimmy and his mom meet people involved in various occupations who are also deaf. Write a letter to a local business asking about its employment policy for people with disabilities. Ask about number of employees, number of employees with disabilities, types of disabilities, job adaptations, and anything else that interests you.

- Gather information about famous people who are deaf or hearing impaired—Johann Sebastian Bach, for example. Share the information with your class in some way—writing, art, music, etc.

 Lakin, P. (1994). *Dad and Me in the Morning*. Morton Grove, IL: Albert Whitman.

The beautiful illustrations and text tell the story of a father and his young son, Jacob, waiting for and enjoying a beautiful sunrise. Jacob just happens to wear hearing aids because he has a hearing impairment. It is clear that Jacob and his dad have a special relationship.

- Jacob's alarm clock flashes to wake him up. With your class, brainstorm a list of modifications that would have to be made for someone with a hearing impairment.

- Jacob and his dad communicate with each other by "signing or lip reading or just squeezing each other's hands." What are some special ways that you communicate with one or both of your parents or another special person in your life? Begin a paragraph, "When I have something _____ (exciting, important, sad, etc.) to say to _____, I _____.

- Look at several photographs or paintings of sunrises. Then paint one of your own or get up very early in the morning and take some photographs.

- Learn a song in sign language and perform it for another class at your school.

 Lee, J. M. (1991). *Silent Lotus.* New York: Farrar, Straus & Giroux.

When Lotus was a little girl she liked to work among the wild birds. Lotus goes with her parents to the city, she sees the temple dancers and wants to dance as they do. But Lotus cannot hear or speak, so her parents aren't sure if the King will give her permission to dance. When he does, Lotus becomes a lovely, graceful dancer who speaks with her hands, body, and feet.

 • Obtain some music for the students to move to as Lotus did.

- Lotus cannot hear, but she can feel vibrations. Feel your throat as you hum. Do you feel vibrations?

- Why is Lotus lonely?

- Lotus learned to speak in a different way. What are some other ways people can "speak" without using their voice? With a partner, try some of these ways.

 Levine, E. S. (1974). *Lisa and Her Soundless World.* New York: Human Sciences Press.

Lisa is a little girl who plays and works like most girls. However, Lisa does not respond to her parents' questions as she should and they discover that she is hearing impaired. The story describes Lisa's learning to converse by wearing a hearing aid, lip reading, and finger spelling. The reader learns the special challenges that are part of living in a silent world.

 • Invite someone from a hearing diagnostics center to show and demonstrate hearing aids.

 • Ask all of the children to sit quietly with their eyes closed for a few minutes. Then make a list of all the sounds they heard.

- Try turning the sound of the television off as you watch a program. Is everything all mixed up like it says in the book?

- Lisa looks very happy when she first gets her hearing aid. Write about a time when you received something that made you very happy.

- Try to see what a friend is saying by reading lips. What problems might Lisa encounter?

- Lisa feels the vibrations that people make when they say a word out loud. With a partner, feel the vibrations made when they say a word.

- Lisa thinks about all the things that she *can* do. Brainstorm a list of all the special things that you can do.

- Lisa is left out sometimes. Write about a time when you were left out.

- After Lisa began using the hearing aid, she discovered many sounds. Go for a walk and listen for sounds you've not heard before.

 Litchfield, A. B. (1976). *A Button in Her Ear.* **Morton Grove, IL: Albert Whitman.**

This delightful book tells the story of Angela and how she came to wear a hearing aid, or "button" in her ear. In different situations, Angela misunderstands what people are saying to her until her parents take her to a doctor to be checked. After she is fitted for the hearing aid, she shows it to her class at school. Her demonstration helps the reader understand the purposes and use of hearing aids.

 • Invite an audiologist to class to explain and demonstrate hearing testing.

 • Invite someone from a hearing diagnostics center to show and demonstrate various types of hearing aids.

 • Invite a speech therapist to talk about the relationship between speech and hearing.

- Angela and Buzzie are friends, but they aren't always nice to each other. Write about a time when you and a friend had trouble getting along.

- Angela's pediatrician examines her ears. Look at an informational picture book that shows the parts of the ear. Learn the name, location, and function of each part.

- Miss Hicks compares Angela's using a hearing aid to wearing glasses to improve vision. List other devices that we use to help us do something better.

- If you were one of the children in Angela's class when she explained her hearing aid, what would you want to ask her?

- Put cotton balls in your ears and then write about the differences you hear.

 Martin, A. (1988). *Jessi's Secret Language.* **New York: Scholastic.**

Jessi is a sixth-grade-girl who, as a member of the Baby Sitters Club, is called upon to babysit for Matt, a child who is deaf. Jessi learns sign language and eventually teaches it to other members of the Baby Sitters Club, as well as using it with Matt. A ballerina, Jessi plans a special event where Matt's sister narrates and Matt's mom interprets for Matt and the other students in his class who are deaf. It is a story of acceptance of those who are different and in addition, the reader learns something about American Sign Language.

 - Obtain instruction on how to sign a few basic phrases using American Sign Language. Teach these to the class.

 - In small groups, make up a secret language or code of your own. Try to have other groups guess your secret message.

- Jessi loves to dance. Tell about a sport or activity you enjoy.

- Why do you think Jessi wanted Haley and Matt to make more friends?

 Peter, D. (1976). *Claire and Emma.* **New York: John Day.**

This book depicts the life of two sisters—Claire, age four, and Emma, age two—who were born deaf. They both wear hearing aids and are involved in lessons that help them speak well. The reader learns of the girls' life with their mother and brother, and their frustrations and victories. This book provides a better understanding of deafness and its implications.

 - Since this book was written, there have been some developments that help deaf people watch TV. Invite someone from a local television station to explain or demonstrate closed captioning.

 - Ask a specialist to explain other advancements for people who are deaf (for example, FM systems, induction loops, etc.).

 - Invite someone from a hearing diagnostics center to show and demonstrate various types of hearing aids.

- The book mentions several things that you can do to help people who are deaf understand. What are these things?

- Keep a record of all the sounds you hear in a school day that give you clues as to the next activity. Discuss your findings with the class and the difficulties that children such as Claire and Emma might have on a given day.

- Claire and Emma are sisters who enjoy doing many things together. Write a letter to your sister, brother, or good friend telling him or her about your favorite things to do together.

- Write a poem about Claire and Emma or just about sisters. Diamante may be a suitable choice for this activity. (See format in Appendix A.)

- With a friend, practice relaying messages using lip reading. What are some of the difficulties you experienced?

Figure 3-3   Examining assistive equipment can help students understand how those with disabilities can be helped.

Peterson, J. W. (1977). *I Have a Sister, My Sister Is Deaf.* **New York: Harper & Row.**

A young girl (the author) tells about her little sister who is deaf. She describes how her sister is like other little girls, and how she is different. Her sister can play the piano, but will never be able to sing because she cannot hear the tune. Her sister does not hear the "sweet tones of the wind chimes," but isn't frightened by loud thunder. The author explains how her sister communicates and how she seems to feel about being deaf. This story is warmly told in black and white sketches and a poetic style.

 • Obtain a copy of the "What's That Sound?" game (Discovery Toys). Play it with your class.

 • Arrange the students to wear sound-blocking headphones for an hour in class. Talk about how it felt not to be able to hear.

• Complete the sentence starter, "I have a sister who . . ." or "I have a brother who . . ." or "I have a friend who . . ."

• Find a partner. Share a pair of sunglasses and take turns talking with them on and off. Is it easier to talk with the glasses on or off? Why?

• Take your journal or some paper and pencils outside. Write down all the sounds you hear. Imagine what it would be like not to hear them.

• How do the two sisters "talk" to each other without using words?

• The two girls sometimes use only their eyes to communicate. Using your eyes, say something to a friend and see if he or she understands you.

• A quote from this book is: "But when she is angry or happy or sad, my sister can say more with her face and her shoulders than anyone else I know." Say something with great feeling using just your face and shoulders. See if a friend knows how you're feeling.

• This is a story of a very special sister. Write a story telling about your sister, brother, or a good friend.

 Rankin, L. (1991). *The Handmade Alphabet.* **New York: Dial Books.**

Laura Rankin presents her creative and striking interpretation of the manual alphabet, one type of signing. The hand that signs "D" holds a delicate dragonfly, "P" dabbles in paint, "M" is reflected in a mirror, "C" holds a dainty teacup—each representation is imaginatively connected to a word that begins with a corresponding letter of the written alphabet.

- Demonstrate signals or gestures to the class. Have them guess what the signal is.

- Learn how to finger spell a particular word or message. With a partner, try to guess the word or message.

- The author's deaf son did not learn to finger spell until he was 18 years old and went to Gallaudet University. Research Gallaudet University in the encyclopedia to find out what is special about it.

- Write to Gallaudet University in Washington DC for information about its programs. You could also visit the Gallaudet University website.

- Select one of the illustrations and write a haiku to go with it. (See format in Appendix A.)

 Ruder-Montgomery, E. (1978). *The Mystery of the Boy Next Door.* **Champaign, IL: Garrard Publishing.**

Joe is a new boy in the neighborhood. He does not respond to the other children when they attempt to talk to him. He rides a different bus to school. When they see him using sign language, the children realize Joe is deaf and vow to learn how to talk to him.

- Joe has a special shirt. Have students design a shirt using fabric paint that tells about themselves.

- Have you ever moved to a new neighborhood? How did you feel?

- Try some of the finger spelling in the back of the book. "Spell" a word to your friend.

- What could you do to welcome a new friend to the neighborhood?

- List the clues that might have led you to think that the new boy was deaf.

- What else could the children have done to get the new boy's attention?

- How did the dog help the boy who was deaf? Find information about dogs that are trained to help the deaf.

- The boy who is deaf probably rides the small bus to a special school for the deaf. If there's a school for the deaf near you, perhaps you could visit.

- What else could the boy do to communicate more effectively?

————————  ————————

 Sullivan, M. B., Bourke, L., & Regan, S. (1980). *A Show of Hands: Say It in Sign Language*. New York: Lippincott.

In largely cartoon format, this book tells the reader about sign language and how it can be modified through the use of body language. It features an interesting section on "Celebrity Signs" (e.g., Hercules signing the word "strong"). Finally, it explains the history of finger spelling and displays the manual alphabet. Children can learn much from the book, as more than 150 signs are shown.

- Have students take turns demonstrating a sign that communicates something and see if other students can identify the message.

- Create some additional "celebrity signers" using crayons, paint, or other media.

- Create a cartoon story similar to those in the book.

- Facial expressions add a lot to hand messages, as well as to what we say when we speak. In small groups, play a game where you say an expression, but use a tone of voice or facial expression that contradicts the message (e.g., say "I'm so happy" in a sad voice). Do the other children know how you feel?

- Learn some of the signs in the book. Teach them to a friend.

- Use facial expressions to convey feelings. Have your friends guess the feeling.

- Sandy describes a perfect day. Write about and illustrate your idea of a perfect day.

- Use finger spelling to say words and short messages.

- Sam tells about why he learned sign language. Write about something important that you learned and tell why you chose to learn it.

- Learn to introduce yourself using sign language. Practice with a friend.

- "How are you feeling?" Practice some of the feeling sentences in sign language with a friend. Try using this communication throughout the day.

————————  ————————

Wheeler, C. (1995). *Simple Signs.* **New York: Penguin Books.**

A tribute to the author's son, this book displays twenty-eight common signs with drawings of children using American Sign Language. "Hints" written at the bottom of each page describe how the gesture is done. Readers learn the signs for words such as "cookie," "butterfly," and "love."

 • Invite an expert to class to explain more about American Sign Language.

• Learn some of the signs in this book. Teach them to a friend.

• Learn to spell your name using finger spelling.

• Examine some of the books listed in the beginning of the book under "Author's Note" for further information on ASL.

 Wolf, B. (1977). *Anna's Silent World.* **Philadelphia: Lippincott.**

Anna was born deaf but she has learned to speak and understand people around her. She is included in a regular first grade classroom and attends a weekly ballet class. She also receives training in lip reading and the use of hearing aids at the New York League for the Hard of Hearing. The text and the black and white photographs tell the story of a wonderful little girl as well as provide specific information about this disability.

 • Invite a speech pathologist to explain how children who are deaf can be taught to talk and lip read.

 • From a diagnostic hearing center, borrow a hearing aid or another type of amplifier such as a "pocket talker" and have children experiment with using it in the classroom.

 • Invite an audiologist to demonstrate and explain how hearing loss is diagnosed.

 • Anna plays a game related to sounds. Acquire a similar game and encourage children to play it in small groups.

• What special considerations might a child who is deaf need in your classroom?

• Anna's family enjoys music and dancing. What are some activities that your family enjoys doing together?

- Anna receives a special gift for Christmas. Tell about a special gift that you have received.

- With a friend, practice relaying messages to each other using lip reading. What difficulties did you experience?

- Anna enjoys swinging during recess. What are your favorite recess activities?

- Anna eats a peanut butter and jelly sandwich for lunch at school. Write a menu that tells about your favorite school lunch.

- Anna enjoys doing special things on Saturdays. Write a journal entry from one of your favorite Saturdays.

- The story ends describing some of Anna's family's Christmas traditions. Write about and/or draw some of the special ways that your family celebrates a holiday.

 Zelonky, J. (1980). *I Can't Always Hear You.* **Milwaukee: Raintree Children's Books.**

Kim, a girl who wears a hearing aid, formerly attended a special school for the hearing impaired. Now she goes to "regular school." When the other students laugh at the way she talks, she wants to go back to her old school. However, with the help of a very understanding teacher and the principal who also wears a hearing aid, Kim is encouraged to stay. Her classmates all share their differences and become friends.

 • Ask a specialist to come in and answer questions about hearing aids (perhaps students could have previously written a letter to Kim asking her questions).

 • How could you welcome a new student to your class? Brainstorm ideas with students.

- Kim's mother said, "Every person has something different about him or her." Discuss with your classmates the differences that you all have.

- How do you think Kim felt when she got in line with the boys to go to the washroom? Write about a time you were embarrassed and what you did about it.

- Ms. Pinkowski, the principal, gave Kim some advice that helps her. She said, "Expect a lot from yourself. Soon others will too." Discuss what she meant by the statement.

- Kim hated being laughed at. Write about a time when someone laughed at you and made you feel uncomfortable or embarrassed.

- Mr. Davis compared his wearing glasses to Kim's wearing a hearing aid. What other devices enable people to do something better?

- Kim talked with her mom about feeling bad that she wore a hearing aid. With whom do you talk when you need to share a problem?

- Why did Mr. Davis suggest that Kim should have laughed too when she discovered herself in the boys' line?

- Make "I'm special because . . ." stickers to share and wear.

CHAPTER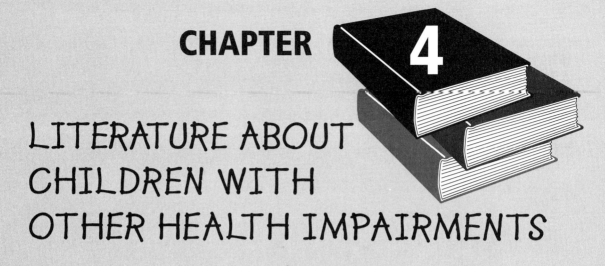

LITERATURE ABOUT CHILDREN WITH OTHER HEALTH IMPAIRMENTS

Children with other health impairments are one of the smaller groups served under the Individuals with Disabilities Education Act (IDEA). According to the Nineteenth Annual Report to Congress on the Implementation of the Individuals with Disabilities Education Act (1997), approximately 133,419 children are identified as having "other health impairments"—three percent of the total number of children with disabilities.

The IDEA definition uses the term "other" to differentiate certain health conditions from those described under physical disabilities involving muscles, joints, and bones (cited in Turnbull, Turnbull, Shank, & Leal, 1995). Specifically, the definition is as follows:

> Having limited strength, vitality, or alertness due to chronic or acute health problems such as heart condition, tuberculosis, rheumatic fever, nephritis, asthma, sickle cell anemia, hemophilia, seizure disorder, lead poisoning, leukemia, or diabetes that adversely affect a child's educational performance. (cited in Turnbull et al., 1995, p. 414)

Prenatal substance exposure, including fetal alcohol syndrome and cocaine/crack manifestations may also qualify as chronic health conditions.

Besides having limitations in strength, vitality, or alertness, individuals with health impairments have few common characteristics. Therefore, we describe the implications for those with AIDS/HIV (identified as a chronic health problem), cancer, asthma, diabetes, and seizure disorders separately. Literature depicting children with these disabilities follows. For the purposes of this text, a few books featuring children with allergies are included in the section on asthma. One selection features separate stories of children with various health impairments. As stated in the *"How to Use This Book"* section, although children with Attention-Deficit Hyperactivity Disorder are commonly served under "Other Health Impairments," Chapter 5 is devoted to this disability.

Acquired Immune Deficiency Syndrome/Human Immunodeficiency Virus (AIDS/HIV)

HIV is a viral disease that breaks down the body's immune system, destroying its ability to fight infections (Caldwell, Todaro, & Gates, 1988). HIV progresses through distinct stages, each marked by increased levels of illness and severity of symptoms. In the final stage, opportunistic infections increase the frequency and severity of symptoms. At this stage, death is usually imminent (Turnbull et al., 1995).

Teachers need to understand how the condition can affect learning and also how to prevent the spread of HIV. Cohen, Mundy, Karassik, Lieb, Ludwig, and Ward (1991) completed a study that indicated that average intellectual functioning can be maintained for many years, even in children with symptoms. However, the study did find some differences in children with HIV in terms of motor speed and attention. It is possible that some special education services might be necessary for some children as the disease progresses (Turnbull et al., 1995).

In terms of the spread of HIV, the use of universal precautions helps prevent the spread through casual contact. The general education classroom is the most appropriate placement for the majority of students with HIV. Those whose behavior or medical condition (for example, biting, open sores) require an alternate setting or who are at risk for infection may receive more individualized instruction through special services.

Cancer

Childhood cancer affected approximately 8,800 children and adolescents in 1997; many suffer from leukemia (American Cancer Society, 1997). Although the survival rate is increasing, some of the treatments may cause a student to miss school frequently. For this reason and others, the American Cancer Society (1988) recommends that all students with cancer have an IEP completed prior to school reentry (cited in Turnbull et al., 1995).

Teachers instructing an individual with cancer should be aware of the condition and the treatments, and should do as much as possible to make sure the child feels included.

Asthma

Asthma is an obstructive lung condition characterized by difficulty in breathing, coughing, wheezing, and·shortness of breath (Caldwell et al., 1988).

Common irritants include smoke, a cold, exercise, cold air, pollen, animal hair, and emotional stress.

Teachers should be aware of the irritants that affect a particular student and of specific procedures for preventing or helping the student in case of an attack. Treatments include managing stress, exercise, and possibly medications such as bronchial dilators (Turnbull et al.,1988).

Juvenile Diabetes

Diabetes is "a disorder of the metabolism caused by an insufficient amount of insulin produced by the body, which results in difficulties digesting and obtaining energy from food" (Hunt & Marshall, 1994, p. 445). Juvenile diabetes occurs before the age of 30. Children with diabetes may monitor their blood glucose levels, control their diet, and give themselves daily injections of insulin (Turnbull et al., 1995).

Teachers should be aware of the particular regimen that a student with diabetes must follow. They should also be aware of the conditions of hyperglycemia (too much sugar) and hypoglycemia (not enough sugar), and the symptoms that indicate each condition. Close supervision of students with diabetes is required.

Seizure Disorder

Seizures are temporary neurological abnormalities that result from unorganized bursts of electrical energy in the brain (Hunt & Marshall, 1994). There are many different types of seizures, some triggered by factors in the environment such as bright lights and sounds. A teacher must be aware of these factors and of appropriate first-aid measures for various types of seizures. It is also imperative to inform peers of first-aid procedures.

REFERENCES

American Cancer Society. (1997). *Cancer facts and figures—1997.* Atlanta: Author.

Caldwell, T., Todaro, A. W., & Gates, A. J. (Eds.). (1988). *Community provider's guide: An information outline for working with children with special needs.* New Orleans: Children's Hospital.

Cohen, C. B., Mundy, T., Karassik, B., Lieb, L., Ludwig, D. D., & Ward, J. (1991). Neuropsychological functioning in human immunodeficiency virus type 1 seropositive children affected through neonatal blood transfusion. *Pediatrics, 88,* 58–68.

Hunt, N., & Marshall, K. (1994). *Exceptional children and youth.* Boston: Houghton Mifflin Company.

Turnbull, A. P., Turnbull, H. R., Shank, M., & Leal, D. (1995). *Exceptional lives: Special education in today's schools.* Englewood Cliffs, NJ: Merrill, an imprint of Prentice Hall.

U.S. Department of Education (1997). Nineteenth annual report to Congress on the implementation of the Individuals with Disabilities Education Act. Washington, DC: U.S. Government Printing Office.

LITERATURE SELECTIONS

Acquired Immune Deficiency Syndrome/Human Immunodeficiency Virus (AIDS/HIV)

 Girard, L.W. (1991). *Alex, the Kid with AIDS.* **Morton Grove, IL: Albert Whitman.**

Alex joins a fourth-grade class where he learns that having AIDS won't get him any privileges if he wants to be a real part of the class. He also finds a best friend. They share a sense of humor, poetry writing, getting in trouble, a sleepover birthday party, their fears, and hopes for many more years.

 • Invite a nurse or a physician in to talk with students about AIDS and universal precautions.

 • Read some poetry with your students: Jack Prelutsky or Shel Silverstein may be a good beginning.

• Some of the children participate in name calling on the playground. Have you ever been called something other than your name? How did it make you feel? What could you do if someone is rude to you?

• The boys write a not-so-nice poem about their teacher. Write a nice poem or a short story about your teacher.

• At first Alex seems to receive special attention from his teacher because he has AIDS. Have you ever received special treatment? Write about or draw a picture of that event.

• Alex hoped to have a sleepover birthday party. Plan a birthday party for yourself, a brother or sister, or a friend. Include the place, games, and activities.

• Write a journal entry from Alex's perspective. You could include your feelings about AIDS, school, friends and your thoughts about the future.

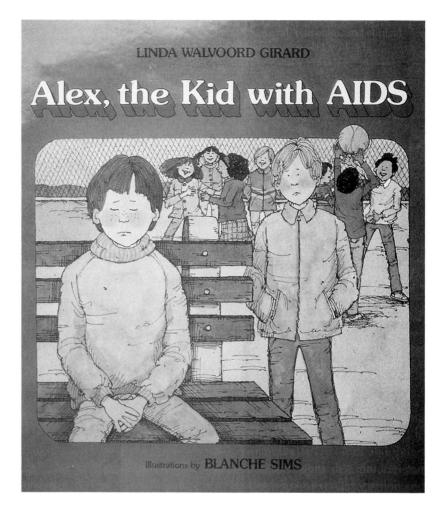

Figure 4-1 *Alex, the Kid with AIDS* by L. W. Girard (1991). Cover reprinted by permission of Albert Whitman.

 Hausherr, R. (1989). *Children and the AIDS Virus*. New York: Clarion Books.

This book discusses the body's immune system, the AIDS virus, and things that can be done to prevent the disease in simple terms that children can understand. The story introduces two children—five-year-old Jonathon and ten-year-old Celeste— who have attended regular schools. The text and photographs help young readers understand the disease, as well as encourage them to treat those with AIDS with compassion.

• Read the "Health Care Precautions" in the back of the book and discuss the use of levels of precaution.

• Write to one of the addresses on p. 44 of the book to find out more about the AIDS virus.

• Write a letter to Jonathon or Celeste. Ask him or her a question you have about the AIDS virus.

• Read "What We Can Do About AIDS" in the back of the book. Think of some other things that you can do about AIDS.

 Merrifield, M. (1990). *Come Sit By Me*. Toronto, Ontario, Canada: Women's Press.

The story begins with a family getting ready to return to school after summer vacation. Karen returns to preschool and makes a new friend, Nicholas. When Nicholas is ill, Karen learns that he has AIDS. She continues to play with Nicholas after her mother explains about AIDS, even though many of the other children's parents have told them not to play with him. Her parents initiate a meeting with parents and teachers to discuss AIDS. The children return to school excited to play with Nicholas again.

 • Invite a pediatrician in to talk about HIV and AIDS.

 • Discuss the picture pages at the end of the book that tell about how someone cannot get AIDS.

• After her first day back at preschool, Karen tells her mom about all that she's done. Write a journal entry or a letter to one of your parents telling about a day at school.

• Many parents told their children not to play with Nicholas. Why did they do that? Why did they change their minds after the meeting?

 Sanford, D. (1989). *David Has AIDS*. Portland, OR: Multnomah.

David is a little boy who has contracted AIDS through a blood transfusion he received because he is a hemophiliac. The book is filled with his prayers to God to help him understand the disease, his fears, and the reason he has to have AIDS. David is comforted by his grandmother who says that "God will be there . . . and you'll have all the light you need." Included in the text is some information about how you can and cannot get AIDS.

 • Discuss ways in which you can and cannot get AIDS. These are outlined in the book.

 • Tell the class about hemophilia.

• David has a special relationship with his grandmother. Tell about a special person in your life.

• This book was written in 1989. Investigate what has been found out about AIDS since then.

• David says that other kids are filled with fear about playing with him and catching AIDS. What could you say to someone who is afraid?

• David has a special toy—a teddy bear. Draw a picture of your favorite toy.

 Schulman, A. (1997). *Carmine's Story: A Book About a Boy with AIDS.* Minneapolis: Lerner Publications.

Carmine is a ten-year-old boy with AIDS, which he contracted at birth from his mother. Carmine lives alone with his grandmother, since his mother died. He shares information about his daily life—things he enjoys, friends he plays with, as well as living with the disease. A photo essay, the book depicts a true story about a boy with a tremendous spirit.

 • Share the "Information About AIDS" section and/or the glossary in the back of the book with the students.

• Carmine's favorite toy is his E.T. doll. Write about or draw your favorite toy. Perhaps bring it to class to share.

• As a class, send balloons up in the sky for Carmine and others who have died from AIDS.

• Write to one of the foundations in the back of the book for information on AIDS.

• Carmine wants to be an actor when he grows up. Tell about what you want to be.

Weeks, S. (1995). *Red Ribbon.* **Hong Kong: A Laura Geringer Book: An Imprint of Harper Collins.**

Written in rhyme, this story tells about a little girl, Jenny, who wonders about the kind of sickness her neighbor has that makes him get "so old so fast." Although she doesn't know him, her mother encourages her to wear a red ribbon in support of the neighbor. Through this book, children understand the significance of the red ribbon as a symbol of hope for those with AIDS. The book comes with an audio cassette that is also called "Red Ribbon."

 • Find out the origin of the red ribbon. Whose idea was it? Why red? After sharing the information with students, make red ribbons for students to wear, put on their desks or lockers, or on a bulletin board.

 • Brainstorm ideas for a class project that could help children with AIDS.

• Wear red ribbons to show your care and hope for people suffering from AIDS.

• Write a poem that encourages people to wear red ribbons in support of people with AIDS. Illustrate your poem.

• What kind of research should scientists do to find effective treatments for AIDS? Find newspaper and news magazine articles about AIDS research.

• Write to one of the two organizations listed in the back of the book that helps adults and children with AIDS.

• Jenny keeps her treasures in a broken cup. Draw some of your treasures and write about where you keep them.

• Bring one of your treasures to class and tell about how it came to be yours and why it's so special.

• Jenny wears a red ribbon to show that she cares. Show someone in your class that you care about him or her.

• Visit a nursing or retirement home. Do something to show you care.

Wiener, L., Best, A., & Pizzo, P. A. (1994). *Be a Friend: Children Who Live with HIV Speak.* Morton Grove, IL: Albert Whitman.

The book presents a compilation of writings and drawings of children with HIV and AIDS. They discuss their hopes and fears and how it feels to be different

Figure 4-2 *Be a Friend: Children Who Live with HIV Speak* by L. Wiener, A. Best, & P. A. Pizzo (1994). Cover reprinted by permission of Albert Whitman.

from other children. All the writings are powerful and very informational in terms of understanding the emotions of children who live with HIV.

- Invite a pediatrician to talk about HIV and AIDS.

- Choose one entry in the book and write a letter to that child, responding to his or her concerns.

- Finish the sentence starter, "I often wonder . . ." with your questions about HIV or AIDS.

- Remember a time when you were ill—perhaps with the flu or chicken pox. Write and illustrate how you felt.

- Damen talks about not being allowed to attend school. Gather some information about Ryan White and share it with your class.

- If you knew that you could only live for one more month, what would you do? List ten things that would be most important to you.

Cancer

Amadeo, D. M. (1989). *There's a Little Bit of Me in Jamie.* **Morton Grove, IL: Albert Whitman.**

Brian and Jamie are brothers who enjoy playing baseball and collecting baseball cards. Jamie is sick with leukemia and is hospitalized for treatments. Brian feels frightened, confused, and neglected by his parents, but finds some comfort when he donates bone marrow to his brother, in the hopes that he can come home again.

- Invite a physician to explain how a bone marrow transplant can help cancer patients.

- Arrange for a field trip to a hospital.

- Why does Brian get so upset when Jamie comes home from the hospital? Have you ever felt neglected by your mom or dad? What did you do?

- Do research to discover how radiation and chemotherapy work on cancer cells.

- Brian gives a special gift to Jamie when he gives him his bone marrow. Write about something special you have done for a brother, sister, or friend.

- Make a card for Jamie when he's in the hospital.

- Write to the National Cancer Society and request information about leukemia.

- Write to the National Bone Marrow Donor program for information about what this group does.

- At one point Brian wishes that he had cancer so that he would get more attention. What do you do when you want more attention? Write a letter to your mom or dad telling them that sometimes you need more attention. Make a short list of things you'd like to do with them.

- Brian gives Jamie his bone marrow. Write about and illustrate something Jamie could give to Brian.

- The story ends with Jamie in the hospital after the bone marrow transplant. Continue the story.

 Bergman, T. (1989). *One Day at a Time: Children Living with Leukemia.* **Milwaukee:** Gareth Stevens.

This is the story of two-year-old Hannah and three-year-old Frederick, both of whom have leukemia. The book describes various treatments for the illness and gives details through vivid but sensitive photographs. The courage with which these children face their illness is inspiring, and the reader realizes that children with leukemia share the hopes and dreams of other children everywhere.

 • Discuss treatments for the disease and how children with cancer need special consideration because of their illness.

 • See "Things to Do and Think About" in the back of the book.

- Write to one of the organizations listed in the back of the book for more information on cancer.

- Design cards for children hospitalized with cancer in your area. Have your teacher deliver them for you.

- Hannah and Frederick are very brave as they face their treatments for leukemia. Tell about a time when you were brave.

- Pretend you are Hannah's or Frederick's brother or sister. What are some things that you could do for them?

Coerr, E. (1993). *Sadako*. New York: G. P. Putnam's Sons.

This is the story of Sadako and her brave fight against leukemia, the "atom-bomb" disease. In hopes of recovery, Sadako tries to make a thousand paper cranes to follow the Japanese legend that the gods will grant a wish to those who can do this. Sadako dies before she can complete the cranes. However, her classmates finish them for her and dream of a monument in Hiroshima to honor her and all of the children killed by the bomb. In 1958, their dream came true.

 • Research what happened in Hiroshima when the atom bomb was dropped. Share your findings with the class.

• Invite a health professional in to talk about leukemia.

• Sadako enjoys running and aspires to be "the best runner in the world." What do you dream of doing?

• Examine the illustrations in *Sadako*. Use watercolors or pastels to create a picture of you pursuing your favorite hobby.

• Read some other legends. Share these with the class.

• Try some simple origami.

 Gaes, J. (1987). *My Book for Kids with Cancer: A Child's Autobiography of Hope*. Aberdeen, SD: Melius and Peterson Publishing.

A heartwarming book, this story recounts the experience of the author, an eight-year-old boy stricken with a rare form of cancer at age six. He describes the tests and treatments, his fears, and hopes. Written in the first person, this book directly addresses the concerns of all children—with and without the disease—regarding cancer.

 • Discuss the concerns of Jason and of the class regarding cancer.

 • Jason describes many treatments he experienced, such as radiation and chemotherapy. Invite a doctor to come to class to explain how these treatments fight cancer.

• Jason lists some of the good things that happen as a result of having cancer. Can you think of any others?

• Design a card for Jason that might make him feel better.

- Make cards for children with cancer who are presently in the hospital. Ask your teacher to deliver these cards for you.

- Jason wants to be a doctor so that he can help kids with cancer. Write about what you want to be when you grow up.

 Krisher, T. (1992). *Kathy's Hats: A Story of Hope.* **Morton Grove, IL: Albert Whitman.**

Kathy's Hats is a wonderful story of a little girl's experience with cancer. It tells of her baby bonnets and the hats she wore for dress-up, Easter, tennis, swimming, baseball, and how hats became an important part of her life during her chemotherapy treatments. Her family and classmates cheer when her treatments end and her cancer goes away. Kathy looks forward to wearing hats for her graduation and wedding when she grows up and picking out hats for a child of her own someday.

 • Read the background of the story, which is included in the book, to the class.

 • Kathy had to undergo chemotherapy treatments. Invite a physician to class to discuss various cancer treatments.

- The story begins when Kathy is a baby. Bring one of your baby photographs to school. Write about something special you did when you were little.

- Kathy wore hats for lots of different activities. Using magazines, catalogs, or newspapers, cut out pictures of hats and people wearing hats. Create a hat collage.

- Kathy collected pins to put on her special hat. Design a pin for her.

- Drawing pictures and watching cartoons sometimes helped Kathy feel better. What do you do to feel better when you are sick?

- Mrs. Hoffman, Kathy's teacher, asked her students to write a story about wishes. Write a poem or story about your special wish.

- Kathy's mother talked with her about the most important hat, a thinking cap. What did she mean by this?

- Kathy's special hat had lots of pins on it. Using fabric, ribbons, lace, etc., decorate a hat.

Figure 4-3   *Kathy's Hats* by T. Krishner (1992). Cover reprinted by permission of Albert Whitman.

Asthma and Allergies

 Bergman, T. (1994). *Determined to Win: Children Living with Allergies and Asthma.* Milwaukee: Gareth Stevens.

This photographic story shows six-year-old Isabel's struggles with asthma and allergies both at home and in a day-care center. The reader becomes aware of the medical treatments and tests used to treat her diseases. Most important, we realize that Isabel is a fighter who wants to be able to go to friends' houses the way her classmates do. The book helps children understand these diseases and be more sympathetic toward children with them.

 • Asthma among children has been increasing in the United States. Invite a health care professional in to discuss this issue.

 • See "Things to Do and Think About" in the back of the book.

 • Isabel and her mother bake a cake. Bake a cake with your class.

 • Play Blind Man's Bluff with your class.

• Do you have any allergies? How are they treated?

• Write to one of the organizations listed on p. 45 for information on allergies and asthma. Report on your findings.

Figure 4-4 *Determined to Win: Children Living with Allergies and Asthma* by T. Bergman (1994). Cover reprinted by permission of Gareth Stevens.

- Do Isabel's diseases slow her down?

- Isabel is allergic to cow's milk. Many people have a lactose intolerance. Gather information from a grocery store and a pharmacy about products that help people deal with this problem.

- Isabel has to spend many spring and summer days indoors. What kinds of things do you enjoy doing when you have to stay indoors? Make a list of activities that Isabel might possibly enjoy.

- Isabel made a little book about herself that included her handprints and footprints. Make a little book about yourself.

 London, J. (1992). *The Lion Who Had Asthma*. Morton Grove, IL: Albert Whitman.

The little boy in this book imagines himself as a hippo, a giant, and a lion. When he has an asthma attack, his mother treats him with a nebulizer and he pretends that he is a pilot until he can breathe easily. He is once again a lion who has a mighty roar.

 • Discuss things that trigger an asthma attack, symptoms, and treatments.

 • Many children have asthma. Invite one of them to describe what happens during an asthma attack.

- Examine a bronchial dilator and have its owner describe when and how it is used.

- Do research on asthma to discover the kinds of irritants that cause asthma attacks.

- The little boy in this story likes to pretend he is a hippo, a giant, and a lion. Do you ever pretend you are something? Write about it.

- Choose an animal and write a description of what it feels like to be that animal. Play charades and have your classmates guess what animal you are.

 Carter, A. R. (1996). *I'm Tougher Than Asthma!* Morton Grove, IL: Albert Whitman.

Siri tells the story of her experience with asthma beginning when she was three. The photographs as well as the text describe her condition and its treatment. Siri explains that she is allergic to animals and house dust mites.

(A photograph of magnified dust mites gives a new perspective on dust.) She considers herself lucky, now that she is not allergic to flowers or weed pollen because she loves to be outdoors. The book also includes "A Note for Parents of Children with Asthma" from Siri's mother, questions/answers about asthma, and additional resources.

 • Invite an allergist in to talk about testing for and treating various allergies.

 • Invite a physician in to talk about the treatment of asthma or invite a child with asthma or the child's parent to talk about their experience with it and to demonstrate a peak flow meter.

 • Acquire a model of the human body so that students can see the lungs.

• Siri begins her story telling about what she likes. Make a list of some of your favorite things. Fit them into an acrostic poem using the letters of your first name. (See format in Appendix A.)

• Use a microscope to view dust particles.

• Siri wants to be a singer and an actress when she grows up. Draw a picture of what you think you want to be when you grow up and what you are doing now to prepare for that.

• Siri is glad that she is not allergic to flower and weed pollen because she loves to be outdoors. Finish the sentence, "I hope I never become allergic to . . . because . . . .

• Siri says that she is tougher than asthma. Have you ever had to "beat" something? Write a short paragraph about that experience and talk with a classmate about it.

 Delson, J. (1985). *I'll Never Love Anything, Ever Again.* Morton Grove, IL: Albert Whitman.

Written in the first person, a boy tells the story of his relationship with his dog Tinsel. He loves Tinsel and knows everything about him and what he likes to do. The doctor says that the boy has to give up Tinsel because he has become allergic to him, and he often misses school due to the allergy. When a family friend offers to take Tinsel, the boy feels a little better and promises to come and visit him soon.

• Make a bar graph of the types and number of pets owned by the children in your class.

• Do you have a special pet like Tinsel? Tell about him. What kinds of things does he like to do?

• Do you have any allergies? Tell about them.

• Imagine how you would feel if you had to give up something you loved. Write about how you might feel.

• Do you think the boy will ever love again?

• Have a pet "show and tell" day when you bring your pets to school. If you cannot bring the pet, bring a picture of the pet to share. (Be sure that no one is allergic to or afraid of animals.)

 Ostrow, W. & Ostrow, V. (1989). *All About Asthma*. Morton Grove, IL: Albert Whitman.

William Ostrow, a young boy, writes of his experience with asthma. His story begins with its discovery and diagnosis at the age of eight when he had his first attack. Different chapters of the book tell what asthma is, what it isn't, what causes it, and how to help oneself. The reader becomes informed about all aspects of asthma through this informational book.

 • Invite an allergist to class to talk about different allergies and how they're diagnosed and treated.

 • Form small groups and ask each to choose one of the eight points under "What Asthma Isn't" and illustrate that point. Hang all the pictures up.

• William begins his story by saying that he's "stuck with asthma." Have you ever felt that you were stuck with something over which you had no control? Write a story about your experience.

• William learned that the number of children with asthma keeps growing as a result of better record keeping and air pollution. Write to the Environmental Protection Agency and ask for information about air pollution in your area and for studies relating to incidence of asthma.

• Write a letter to William. His address is on the last page.

• Asthma and allergies seem to be inherited. Talk with your family about physical characteristics that have been inherited in your family.

- One of William's suggestions is keeping a diary of the things he eats. Do the same and note how you feel afterward.

- Dust isn't good for anyone. Go home and dust the things in your room.

- William's friend suggests that he should imagine himself in his favorite place when he's having an attack. Close your eyes and imagine your favorite place. Does it help you relax? Draw a picture of the place and put it somewhere special.

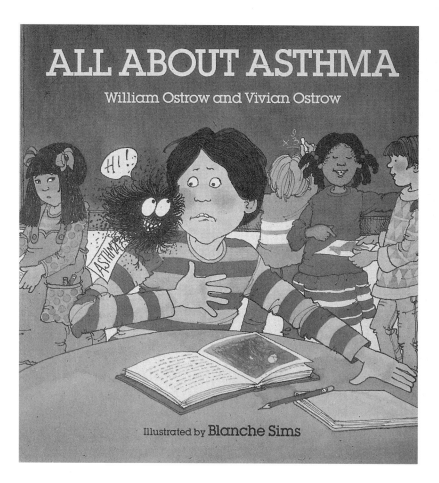

Figure 4-5 *All About Asthma* by W. Ostrow & V. Ostrow (1989). Cover reprinted by permission of Albert Whitman.

Rogers, A. (1987). *Luke Has Asthma, Too.* Burlington, VT: Waterfront Books.

This is the story of a little boy who has asthma. He admires his older cousin, Luke, who also has asthma. One day, the boy's asthma doesn't respond to medicine as it should, and he goes to the hospital. There they teach both him and his parents about asthma and what to do for it. Through this book, the reader comes to better understand this illness.

- Discuss the implications for those with asthma in the classroom situation.

- Write to one of the organizations listed in the back of the book to obtain more information about asthma.

- The boy in the story admires his older cousin Luke. Tell about someone you admire.

- The boy's dad brings his special pajamas and toys to the hospital, which make him feel better. What special toys would make you feel better if you were the boy?

- Is Luke a good friend to the boy? Why?

Juvenile Diabetes

 Bates, B. (1988). *Tough Beans.* New York: Holiday House Books.

Nat Berger is a fourth-grade student who has just found out that he has diabetes. The beginning of the book details him learning about his condition and how to treat it. Nat, with the help of his friend Cassie, begins to accept his condition and take charge of his life. With this discovery, he even learns how to handle Jasper, the fourth-grade bully, and that there are worse things than diabetes.

- Invite a physician to class to explain more about diabetes and show a gly-cometer—the instrument used by Nat to check his sugar level.

- Nat had not been feeling well for some time prior to going to the hospital in the beginning of the book. What are some of the symptoms of diabetes the book describes?

- Cassie is a special friend to Nat and he is sad when he has to move away. Tell about a special friend of yours.

- Do you think the fact that Nat's teacher also is a diabetic will help Nat? Why?

- Why do you think Jasper took the candy bar from Nat's pocket?

- The book explains that there is no "cure" for diabetes. Write a letter to a researcher explaining the importance of continued research on diabetes.

 Peacock, C. A., Gregory, A., & Gregory, K. C. (1998). *Sugar Was My Best Food: Diabetes and Me*. Morton Grove, IL: Albert Whitman.

Adair tells the story of how he was diagnosed with diabetes and how he got better. He explains blood levels, insulin, giving shots, meal plans, giving up sugar—especially candy, and how all of it feels. Working together, Adair, his family, friends, teachers, and physician help him regain his life and even compete in track. This is a true story and Adair Gregory promises to answer every letter that he receives.

- Adair explained diabetes to his class. Make a list of what students know about diabetes after reading the book and what they'd still like to know. Prepare questions that could be answered through research or by a physician.

- Invite a health care professional in to talk about diabetes and to demonstrate the fingertip blood testing and injections using an orange.

- Adair begins his story by describing himself and his family. Write a similar description of yourself and your family.

- Sugar was Adair's best food. He "lived for candy." His favorite holiday was Halloween. What is your best food and your favorite holiday?

- Before Adair got sick, he and his father took a special outing every Saturday. What do you enjoy doing with one of your parents or another important adult?

- Adair's eating became very scheduled. For one week, keep track of everything you eat and the time of day that you eat. Analyze your eating habits. Was that week typical or unusual? Write a paragraph.

- The week before fourth grade began, Adair's mom arranged a meeting with his teacher to tell her about the diabetes. Write a letter to your teacher telling him/her some things that you think are important to know about you.

- Adair can have very little sugar. Make a list of foods that you think he'd like that are sugarless.

- Create a Venn diagram depicting the similarities and differences between you and Adair.

- Write a letter to Adair or e-mail him at the address he provides on the last page.

Figure 4-6   Character analysis can be aided through the use of Venn diagrams.

 Pirner, C. W. (1991). *Even Little Kids Get Diabetes.* **Morton Grove, IL: Albert Whitman.**

In this story, the little girl tells of her diagnosis of diabetes when she was two years old and the daily treatment she has to face. She explains how she has to check regularly to see if she has too much or too little insulin. The reactions of her family are also explained.

 • The title, *Even Little Kids Get Diabetes*, tells one important fact about diabetes. Juvenile diabetes happens to children. Invite a physician to talk to the class about juvenile and adult diabetes.

• The little girl in the book says she was scared when she had to go to the hospital. Write about a time when you were scared.

• Even the cat and dog look scared when the little girl has to have her shot. Would you be scared to have a daily shot?

• Read the letter from the author in the back of the book. Does it sound like diabetes has limited her daughter's life?

Connie White Pirner

Even Little Kids Get Diabetes

pictures by Nadine Bernard Westcott

Figure 4-7   *Even Little Kids Get Diabetes* by C. W. Pirner (1991). Cover reprinted by permission of Albert Whitman.

 Roy, R. (1982). *Where's Buddy?* New York: Clarion Books.

> Buddy is a seven-year-old boy who has diabetes. Mike, his brother, is responsible for watching him one afternoon and making sure that he gets his insulin shot at the right time. However, Buddy disappears with a friend and Mike must frantically search for him along the rocky Maine coast. Buddy is found

and both boys learn some important lessons about responsibility. Through this book, the reader comes to understand some of the manifestations of diabetes, as well as enjoy a suspenseful story.

 • Invite a physician to class to further explain this illness.

• How do you think Mike felt when he could not find Buddy?

• Mike was responsible for Buddy. What are some things you are responsible for?

• Continue the story. How will Mike and Buddy work together in the future?

Seizure Disorders

 Moss, D. M. (1989). *Lee, the Rabbit with Epilepsy.* Kensington, MD: Woodbine House.

Lee's epilepsy is discovered after she experiences her first seizure while she's fishing with her grandfather. Her doctor explains epilepsy and different types of seizures and prescribes medication. Lee realizes that she can still do anything she wants, including fishing. This book is part of a series of special needs books written for children.

 • Gather information from students about whether they've ever gone fishing, where, and what they caught.

 • Invite a parent who fishes or someone from a sports equipment store to show various fishing paraphernalia and demonstrate the sport.

 • Invite an adult who has epilepsy to talk to the class and describe what it feels like, medication, etc.

 • Invite the school nurse or another health professional to explain and demonstrate what to do for someone who has a seizure.

• "Dr. Bob" explains that there are different types of epileptic seizures and prescribes medication for Lee's kind of epilepsy. Ask the school nurse or another health professional to discuss this condition.

• Lee's grandfather insisted that Lee try fishing again. Why do you think he did that?

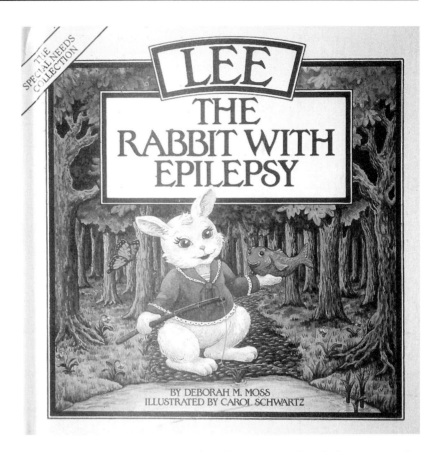

Figure 4-8 *Lee, the Rabbit with Epilepsy* by D. M. Moss (1989). Cover reprinted by permission of Woodbine House.

- Lee enjoyed fishing with her grandfather. Write about and illustrate something that you enjoy doing with a grandparent or someone else who is special to you.

- Do you think Lee will be afraid to fish or do other activities in the future?

Multiple Illness

 Berger, L. & Litwick, D. (1992). *I Will Sing Life: Voices from the Hole in the Wall Gang Camp*. Boston: Little, Brown.

        The book unveils stories of seven children from ages seven to seventeen, who are combating life-threatening illnesses such as cancer, leukemia, and AIDS.

They reflect on the importance of their families and friends, and confront their future with astounding courage. The reflections are enhanced through poetry written by the children and pictures of their daily lives.

 • Discuss how each of the children in this book displays courage.

 • Many of the children in the book write poetry. Prepare a poetry writing experience.

 • In cooperative groups, have the children research the illnesses presented in the book and share findings with the class.

• What do you think the title, "I Will Sing Life" means?

• The children in this book all go to a special camp. Have you ever been to camp or similar place? Tell about what you did there.

• Design a card for one of the children in this book.

CHAPTER 5

LITERATURE ABOUT ATTENTION-DEFICIT HYPERACTIVITY DISORDER

As mentioned in Chapter 4 on "Other Health Impairments," the authors of this text have opted to devote a single chapter to literature about children with Attention-Deficit Hyperactivity Disorder (ADHD). The potential opportunity for teachers to readily access books on this topic warranted a separate chapter.

It has been difficult to decide where to classify students with ADHD under the Individuals with Disabilities Education Act (IDEA). One reason is because of the frequent association and overlap of ADHD with learning disabilities and serious emotional disturbances. Technically, under a 1991 memorandum issued by the U.S. Department of Education, students with ADHD *and* another diagnosis can receive services for both under the other diagnosis. Those with ADHD who do not have another diagnosis can still receive services under "Other Health Impairments" if the condition affects their educational performance (cited in Lerner, Lowenthal, & Lerner, 1995).

According to the *Diagnostic and Statistical Manual of Mental Disorders* (1994), there are three types of ADHD with associated symptoms:

1. Predominantly inattentive type—students who have trouble paying attention in class and are easily distracted. Possible symptoms include failure to give close attention to details or making careless mistakes, difficulty sustaining attention in tasks or play activities, not listening, not following through on instruction, difficulty organizing tasks and activities, avoiding tasks that require sustained mental effort, losing things, easy distraction by extraneous stimuli, and forgetfulness. Children diagnosed with this type of ADHD have at least six of these symptoms that have persisted for at least six months.

2. Predominantly hyperactive-impulsive type—students who cannot seem to sit still, often talk excessively, and find playing quietly difficult. Possible symptoms of hyperactivity include fidgeting with hands or feet, leaving his/her seat in the classroom, running or climbing excessively in situations where it is inappropriate, having difficulty playing or engaging in leisure activities quietly, talking excessively, acting as if "driven by a motor," and showing an inability to sit still. Symptoms of impulsivity include blurting out answers to questions, difficulty waiting in lines or awaiting turns, and interrupting or intruding on others. Children diagnosed with this type of ADHD have at least six of these symptoms that have persisted for at least six months.

3. Combined type—students with a combination of both types. Children diagnosed with this type of ADHD have at least six symptoms of inattention and six symptoms of hyperactivity.

In addition to these symptoms, the following additional criteria must be met: onset of symptoms no later than the age of seven; symptoms present in two or more situations; significant distress or impairment in social, academic, or occupational functioning; in addition, the symptoms do not occur exclusively during the course of a pervasive developmental disorder or schizophrenia or other psychotic disorders and are not better accounted for by a mood disorder, anxiety disorder, dissociative disorder, or personality disorder (cited in Lerner, Lowenthal, & Lerner, 1995).

There are many implications for the child with ADHD in the inclusive classroom. According to Fouse and Morrison (1997), teachers may have unrealistic expectations for these students that often sets them up for failure. The children may think that "there is no point in trying because their efforts rarely seem to make a difference" (Fouse & Morrison, 1997, p. 442). Students with the inattentive type have many problems academically, and are often rejected socially because they tend to withdraw from others. Those with the hyperactive-impulsive type tend to be disruptive and may be socially rejected because of this reason; they also have academic difficulties in the classroom.

Teachers must be aware of behavior management techniques as well as have knowledge of medical management and psychological counseling techniques that may be prescribed for a particular child. The teacher must have realistic expectations for all of these interventions with respect to the classroom performance of the child. Teachers, parents, and medical personnel must communicate regularly about progress made.

Several literature selections featuring children with ADHD follow. They inform the reader of the character's feelings about the disorder and also present potential treatment options. Those with ADHD can have a productive life, both inside and outside of the classroom.

REFERENCES

American Psychiatric Association. (1994). *Diagnostic and statistical manual of mental disorders*. (4th ed.). Washington, DC: Author.

Fouse, B., & Morrison, J. A. (1997). Using children's books as an intervention for attention deficit disorder. *The Reading Teacher, 50*(5), 442-445.

Lerner, J. W., Lowenthal, A., & Lerner, S. R. (1995). *Attention deficit disorders: Assessment and teaching*. Pacific Grove, CA: Brooks/Cole Publishing Company.

LITERATURE SELECTIONS

 Caffrey, J. A. (1997). *First Star I See*. Fairport, NY: Verbal Images Press.

Paige Bradley, a fourth grader, struggles to pay attention in class, complete homework, and keep her school supplies organized. She is reluctant to deal with her Attention Deficit Disorder (ADD), as her younger brother has been diagnosed with the hyperactive type. Paige desperately wants to win a writing contest so that she can meet Dr. Kelsey Strongheart, an actress from her favorite television show, *Star Warriors*. With the support of Mr. Rodriguez, the assistant principal, Paige's imagination and her knowledge of astronomy come together successfully.

 • *Star Warriors* is "the most awesome TV show ever," according to Paige. Ask students, "What is your favorite television program?" Do a survey of the class and display the information in a graph.

 • Mr. Rodriguez is an amateur astronomer and has a telescope in his office. Arrange a field trip to a planetarium.

 • One of Paige's most embarrassing moments was when she was caught decorating her math quiz answer sheet. Have students work in pairs and talk about embarrassing moments. They will realize that everyone has them and survives them.

 • This book connects well with a unit of study on astronomy. Students could develop individual projects similar to those required by Paige's teacher.

• Paige was sent to see the assistant principal. If you could have a conversation with your principal, what would you want to talk about? Write a note or letter to your principal telling him/her something special about yourself.

- Because Paige's parents are divorced, she does separate things with each of them. List or draw the activities that you enjoy doing with each of your parents or with someone special to you.

- Paige sometimes finds herself daydreaming. When do you daydream? What do you think about? Write about or draw your favorite daydream.

- Paige's favorite place to daydream is an old tree in her front yard. Write a poem about your favorite place to daydream.

- Paige's brother has ADHD. Make a Venn diagram showing the similarities and differences in their conditions.

- Paige has a hard time getting her project organized and started. Make a list of suggestions that would have been helpful to her.

- Paige creates the visual part of her project in the garage. Draw or paint a picture or create a diorama illustrating what you think Paige's project looked like.

Figure 5-1 Art activities can enhance a story.

- Paige's project was destroyed by her dog when her brother Mark forgot to close the garage door. What would you have done in Paige's situation? Write or tape record the "conversation" you would have with your brother, mother, and/or teacher.

- Because Paige had not followed the rules for the project by not submitting her outline on time, she was not allowed to present her paper at the school assembly even though it was the best. Do you think that was a fair decision?

- Mr. Rodriguez talks with Paige about seeing "the big picture." What does he mean? Was it fair that Paige got to meet Renee La Straps, Dr. Kelsey, her television heroine?

 Corman, C. L., & Trevino, E. (1995). *Eukee, the Jumpy Jumpy Elephant.* **Plantation, FL: Specialty Press.**

Eukee is an elephant who can't pay attention in school and therefore gets in trouble all the time. He goes to visit "Dr. Tusk" and tells him his problems. Dr. Tusk runs some tests and explains that Eukee feels "jumpy" all the time because he has Attention Deficit Disorder (ADD). Eukee gets the help he needs and begins to do better in school.

- Invite a health professional to explain ADD.

- Eukee shakes the trees and branches with force and doesn't finish the elephant march because he is distracted. Have you ever felt distracted? What helps you pay attention?

- What kind of behavior chart might Eukee follow? Devise one.

 Galvin, M. (1995). *Otto Learns About His Medicine.* **New York: Magination Press.**

The story uses the metaphor of a car whose engine runs too fast to explain the effects of Attention-Deficit Hyperactivity Disorder. Otto's "mechanic" prescribes a medicine that helps him focus and pay attention. Otto's questions and the answers about the condition and his medication help the reader understand the implications of ADHD.

- Invite a medical specialist to come and discuss medications used to treat ADHD and the possible side effects.

- Did you ever feel like Otto—have a hard time paying attention in school?

- Why did the author and illustrator of this book choose a car to describe this condition?

- What could the teacher and Otto's classmates do to help him in school?

- Dramatize this story.

 Gehret, J. (1991). *Eagle Eyes: A Child's Guide to Paying Attention.* Fairport, NY: Verbal Images Press.

Ben tells the story of an outing with his family. As the family tries to feed the birds, Ben scares the birds away because he is so clumsy. At school, he can't seem to get his homework done. Ben finally finds out that he has Attention Deficit Disorder (ADD). His dad explains that he has "eagle eyes"—that he notices everything, but can't tune out some things. He learns ways that help him focus more. In the end, Ben's eagle eyes help his family when they are lost in the wilderness on another outing; Ben is the only one who can find his way back.

 • In the back of the book are symptoms of Attention Deficit Disorder. Discuss these and problems that children with ADD might encounter.

- Ben is compared to an eagle because he notices a lot of things. What animal might you be compared to? Draw a picture of the animal. Explain your choice.

- Write your story of a family outing or an activity you have done with friends.

- Ben has to take medication for Attention Deficit Disorder. Find out more about what this medication does to help those with ADD.

- Ben can't find his coat before going to school and, as a result, misses the bus. Make a list of things that you can do the night before to prepare for school in the morning.

- Ben's nickname was Eagle Eyes because he noticed everything. Go for a nature walk, perhaps with a guide. When you return, write down or draw five interesting things that you saw.

Gehret, J. (1992). *I'm Somebody Too.* **Fairport, NY: Verbal Images Press.**

Told from the perspective of an almost twelve-year-old girl, Ginny reflects on growing up with her younger brother who has Attention Deficit Disorder (ADD). Issues of growing up, friends, and school are intertwined with a family's successful dealing with a child who has ADD.

 • Arrange for a pediatrician or counselor to discuss ADD with the class.

 • Arrange for a horseback riding field trip or visit a horse farm or riding stable.

• Emily and Ginny are best friends at the beginning of the book, but that changes. Why do you think that happened? Have you "changed friends"? How did that feel? Write a short letter to a new friend.

• Dr. Lawson recommended that Emily's family do something fun together. Plan an outing for your family. Include cost, special equipment, etc.

• Emily sometimes felt like her doll with two faces. Draw the two faces and then write underneath what each might say to your mom, dad, sister, brother, friend, or teacher.

• Try some of the activities in the "Epilogue: Surviving the Storm" at the end of the book.

 Gordon, M. (1991). *Jumpin' Johnny, Get Back to Work! A Child's Guide to ADHD.* **Dewitt, NY: GSI.**

Johnny just can't sit still. He has a hard time in school and often gets into trouble at home, too. Finally, Johnny goes to a psychologist who tells him he has Attention-Deficit Hyperactivity Disorder (ADHD). He also finds out from his parents that he isn't the first in the family with ADHD. With suggestions from the doctor and some medications, Johnny can pay attention much easier at school and at home.

 • Invite a health specialist to speak about medications for people with ADHD.

 • Ask an older student with ADHD to speak to the class about growing up with this disability.

• Johnny calls his sister "Little Miss Wonderful." Is there a special name you call a brother, sister, or friend? Write a short story explaining the name.

- Draw a picture of yourself doing something with your brother or sister that you both enjoy.

- Johnny's teacher has special rules and rewards for following the rules. What is done in your classroom to promote good behavior?

- Make a special sign on the computer for a friend.

 Gordon, M. (1992). *My Brother's a World Class Pain*. DeWitt, NY: GSI Publications.

In this story, a girl tells about her younger brother, Timmy, who can't sit still, often spills things and is an "accident waiting to happen." Timmy is finally diagnosed as having Attention-Deficit Hyperactivity Disorder (ADHD). The family sees a psychologist who helps them with how to help Timmy and Timmy also starts on some medication. This story introduces readers to many of the basic concepts involved in understanding ADHD.

 - Invite a physician to explain more to the class about ADHD.

 - Take a poll of the types of chores the children do at home. Graph your results.

- Sometimes Timmy is a "world-class pain," according to the girl. Do you have a brother or sister or friend who sometimes does things that bother you? Tell about it.

- How might Timmy be helped at school?

 Janover, C. (1997). *Zipper, the Kid with ADHD*. Bethesda, MD: Woodbine House.

Zipper is a fifth grade boy who displays symptoms of Attention-Deficit Hyperactivity Disorder (ADHD) both at home and at school. He forgets to do his homework. He speaks before he thinks and he can't sit still. His impulsiveness even leads him to steal a magazine from a store. At wits end, his parents and teacher help him deal with his condition. Zipper gathers the courage to overcome his problem and in his words, "make it big."

 - Read and discuss the appendix in the back of the book with the class.

 - Invite a physician in to explain more about causes, symptoms, and treatment of ADHD.

- On p. 25, the simile, "thoughts bounced in his head like a pinball machine," describes Zipper's thinking. Use another simile to describe something. Illustrate your simile.

- Zipper is Zach's nickname. Do you have a nickname you like to be called? Write an acrostic poem using your name or nickname. (See format in Appendix A.)

- Zach plays drums, which helps him channel his physical energy. What else could he do?

- Zach really enjoys playing baseball. What sport or activitiy do you enjoy?

- Making a list is one way that Zach organizes his thoughts. Try making a list of "things to do" yourself. Does it help you?

 Moss, D. M. (1990). *Shelley the Hyperactive Turtle*. Bethesda, MD: Woodbine House.

This is the story of Shelley, a turtle who continues to do "bad" things, even though he wants to "be good more than anything in the world." Shelley goes to a doctor who runs tests and tells him that he is "hyperactive." The doctor prescribes medicine that helps him. As he grows, Shelley feels less wiggly and jumpy inside.

- Brainstorm lists of "good" and "bad" things that children do at school. Discuss the importance of good manners and kindness.

- Why do you think Shelley does bad things even though he wants to be good?

- Have you ever done bad things even though you were trying to be good?

- If Shelley were in your class, what could you do to help him?

- Usually turtles are thought to be slow, but in this book, Shelley is described as hyperactive. Write and illustrate a story about another animal that displays characteristics different than you would expect.

 Peters, T. (1996). *Hip-Hop the Hyperactive Hippo*. Gladstone, NJ: Tim Peters and Co.

Hip-Hop is a young hippo who can't seem to slow down and disturbs all the other animals with his splashing and running. He and his parents visit Dr. Rhino, who says he has Attention-Deficit Hyperactivity Disorder (ADHD),

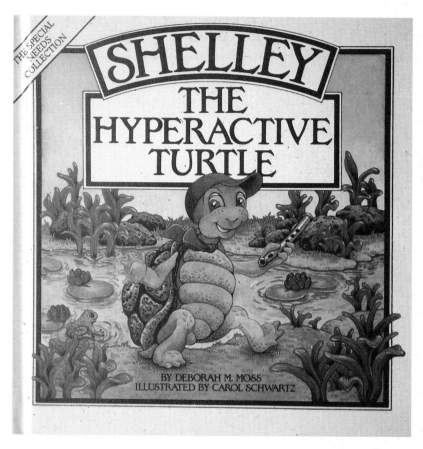

Figure 5-2   *Shelley, the Hyperactive Turtle* by D. M. Moss (1990). Cover reprinted by permission of Woodbine House.

and helps him with some activities that will allow Hip-Hop to do his best. The doctor tells Hip-Hop that the activities alone will not change his behavior—only he can do that.

- Expand on the information section on the last page in a discussion with the class about ADHD.

- Dr. Rhino says that he will help Hip-Hop by giving him some tricks and activities to allow him to do his best. What do you think he was talking about?

- Continue the story. Will everything be "just fine" for Hip-Hop?

- Write a story using animals for main characters. Illustrate your story.

CHAPTER 6

LITERATURE ABOUT CHILDREN WITH MENTAL RETARDATION

In 1993, the definition of mental retardation as developed by the American Association on Mental Retardation (AAMR) was adopted as the federal definition. The definition consists of three parts: 1) significantly subaverage intellectual functioning, existing concomitantly with 2) limitations in two or more adaptive skill areas: communication, self-care, home living, social skills, community use, self-direction, health and safety, functional academics, leisure, and work, and 3) manifestations before age eighteen (cited in Hunt & Marshall, 1994).

To expand upon the definition, the phrase "subaverage intellectual functioning" refers to performance on one or more intelligence tests resulting in an IQ of about 70 or below. However, as indicated in the definition, the subaverage intellectual functioning must exist concomitantly with limitations in adaptive behavior. In other words, a student with an IQ of 65 who has good adaptive behavior may not be identified as having mental retardation, whereas a student with an IQ score of 75 who has poor adaptive behavior may be identified as such. The definition of what constitutes "adaptive behavior" varies according to the developmental level of the child. Adaptive behavior provides a more comprehensive picture of the child's abilities than IQ alone. The element of "manifestation before age 18" is included in the definition to distinguish mental retardation from conditions in which adults suffer impairment in brain functioning, such as due to a stroke.

According to the Nineteenth Annual Report to Congress on the Implementation of the Individuals with Disabilities Education Act (1997), approximately 585,308 children between the ages of six and twenty-one are identified as having mental retardation—twelve percent of the total number of children with disabilities. There are various classifications to denote degrees of mental retardation. Commonly accepted terms include "mild," "moderate," "severe," and "profound." Each category generally has more inclusive academic, intellectual, social, and adaptive problems. The vast majority—eighty to eighty-five percent of those with mental retardation— fall into the "mild" group and are integrated into the community. The smaller percentage of those with moderate, severe, or profound retardation need much more support and direction.

The school curriculum varies for included students with mental retardation, depending upon the severity of the condition. Overall, the focus may be developmental (normally presented scope and sequence of skills), functional (basic skills taught in the context of real life or community activities), or remedial (alleviating a deficit) (Hardman, Drew, & Winston-Egan, 1996). Many of the instructional methods used for all students, such as peer tutoring, cooperative learning, establishing clear goals and expectations, and praise/reinforcement of success are also appropriate for students with mental retardation. Because vast differences exist among those with mental retardation, it is critical to consider the needs of each individual when planning an appropriate academic curriculum.

In any case, social skills may need to be taught directly since they are a vital part of the educational experience for many students with mental retardation. These students often do not learn such skills incidentally (Polloway & Patton, 1993). Working with the students without disabilities on appropriate responses to and/or interactions with the child with mental retardation is also important. Peers can be given the responsibility for helping select and practice appropriate social behavior with those students who need it. Pairing students to participate in various classroom activities is another way to promote socialization among all students.

The literature selections depict children with mental retardation in a variety of roles. Readers become aware of the challenges that face children with mental retardation both in the school setting and in everyday life. More important, however, is the underlying theme in many of the books that those with mental retardation have the same experiences and needs as other children in their age group.

REFERENCES

Hardman, M. L., Drew, C. J., Winston-Egan, M. (1996). *Human exceptionality: Society, school, and family* (5th ed.). Boston: Allyn & Bacon.

Hunt, N., & Marshall, K. (1994). *Exceptional children and youth.* Boston: Houghton Mifflin.

Polloway, E. A., & Patton, J. R. (1993). *Strategies for teaching learners with special needs.* (6th ed.) Columbus, OH: Merrill.

U.S. Department of Education. (1997). Nineteenth annual report to Congress on the implementation of the Individuals with Disabilities Education Act. Washington, DC: U.S. Government Printing Office.

LITERATURE SELECTIONS

 Anders, Rebecca. (1976). *A Look at Mental Retardation.* Minneapolis: Lerner Publications.

The text and photographs describe problems faced by people who have mental retardation. Causes of mental retardation, identification, and ways that others can help those with mental retardation are explained in clear, easy-to-understand terms.

- Invite a pediatrician to class to talk about healthy minds and bodies as well as more specific causes of mental retardation (drugs, etc.).

- We all have special abilities and talents. Write about your special gift. Include an illustration.

- With a partner, list some ways you could help a child with mental retardation if he or she were in your class.

- Write a letter to a friend that summarizes the information presented about mental retardation in the book.

- What are some very important things that people with mental retardation should learn? Make a list.

 Becker, S. (1991). *Buddy's Shadow.* Hollidaysburg, PA: Jason & Nordic Publishers.

Buddy, a five-year-old boy with Down syndrome, has a hard time keeping up with other children his age because he can't run as fast. Buddy saves his money for a puppy—his best friend. The dog, Shadow, can run faster than anybody, and Buddy discovers that running fast just doesn't matter among friends.

- Encourage a discussion of friendship and how differences can enhance a relationship among friends.

- Buddy probably felt left out when he watched Janie and the other children play. Write about a time when you felt left out.

- Write a letter to Buddy telling him about your pet or a special toy.

- Was Shadow a good name for the dog? If you have a pet, tell how he or she got his or her name.

———————— ✂ ————————

 Bergman, T. (1989). *We Laugh, We Love, We Cry: Children Living with Mental Retardation.* Milwaukee: Gareth Stevens.

The book tells the story of two sisters, Asa and Anapa Karin. That both have the same disability, which includes mental retardation. The black and white illustrations and text describe the home life, physical therapy, and schooling of these two special girls.

 • Invite a physical therapist and occupational therapist to talk to the class about their work.

Thomas Bergman

Figure 6-1 *We Laugh, We Love, We Cry* by T. Bergman (1989). Cover reprinted by permission of Gareth Stevens.

• See "Things to Do and Talk About" on page 45.

• The book says that many children with disabilities must be more independent than other children. Write about a time when you had to be independent.

• Many children with disabilities realize more than others might think. How might this information help you as you get to know them?

• There are questions in the back of the book. What other questions do you have?

 Berkas, C. W. (1992). *Charlsie's Chuckle.* **Rockville, MD: Woodbine House.**

Charlsie is a little boy with Down syndrome whose wonderful chuckle makes his family and those around him smile. The story focuses on a Town Council meeting that involves a heated discussion about the town's problems. Charlsie's chuckle saves the day. Although Charlsie is unable to tell his mom about the exciting event, she happily reads about it in the newspaper.

 • Charlsie has a wonderful chuckle and chuckles at many things. Have the children make a list of things that make them laugh. They could write and illustrate a class book or make individual books about what makes them laugh.

 • Invite a member of the Town Council to talk with students about their work and the issues they discuss.

 • There is some information in the back of the book about Down syndrome. Invite a medical professional to speak further about Down syndrome.

 • Laugh. Take two minutes and encourage everyone to laugh. Listen to everyone's different laughs.

• Read newspaper articles about Town Council meetings in your city.

• Tell about a time when you made someone very proud of you.

• Sometimes people use funny expressions to describe other people. For example, look at what was done on p. 13 of this book. Choose one of those expressions or a different one, and draw a picture of what you would imagine that person to look like (such as a woman with "bees in her bonnet").

Booth, Z. (1987). *Finding a Friend.* Mt. Desert, ME: Windswept House.

Andy and Mike are both eight years old and become the best of friends when Mike's family moves to the orchard to manage the workers. Mike has mental retardation, yet enjoys doing most of the things that Andy likes to do. One adventure they have is the discovery of their "secret" cave. One day Andy disappears and everyone searches for him. Mike thinks to check the cave. It is because of Mike that Andy is discovered with a broken leg and is rescued from the cave.

- Lead the class in a discussion of friendship. As a class, write an acrostic poem using the word "friendship." (See format in Appendix A.)

- Andy and Mike are good friends. Tell what you like to do with one of your friends.

- Why do some children tease people with disabilities? Why did children in this story tease Andy also?

- Andy says that Mike sometimes has "stubborn spells." Why is this?

- Do you have a secret place where you can go?

- Andy and Mike had a disagreement at their swimming lesson. What do you do if you have a disagreement with a friend?

 Brightman, A. (1976). *Like Me.* Boston: Little, Brown.

In poetic form, a little boy who has mental retardation looks at the word "retarded" and what it means. He examines many friends like him who, although they are slow, are like other children in most ways. As he states, the word is just a word, "a kid is much more than a word." The photographs, which depict many children, are very endearing.

- This story is written as a poem. Instruct the students in writing a poem about the ways that they and their friends are alike and different.

- Using a photograph, make a bulletin board of each classmate. Let each child write something that he or she likes to do under the photograph.

- With a partner, make a Venn diagram of ways in which you are different and ways in which you are the same.

- The little boy in the book says he likes to be alone sometimes because he can say what he wants. Do you like to be alone sometimes?

- Fold a paper into four squares. Draw one thing from the book that you remember in each of the squares. Choose one of the squares and write a description of it.

- Select a word—happy, sad, fun, exciting, scary—and create a collage cut from magazine pictures to illustrate that word.

- Make a list or draw pictures of things that you do well. Name several things that you'd like to learn to do or learn to do better.

- See "A Personal Note" at the end of the book from the author.

 Carter, A. R. (1997). *Big Brother Dustin*. Morton Grove, IL: Albert Whitman.

This is a delightful photo essay of Dustin's wait for his new baby sister. Dustin helps prepare for the baby and tries to think of names for her. He is the one who names her Mary Ann after his two grandmothers. Dustin has Down syndrome, but no mention is made of it in the story.

 - Have students gather information about classmates' favorite names for boys and girls. Display the information on a graph.

- Has there been a new baby in your family recently? Were you as excited as Dustin?

- Find out who chose your name and why you were given it.

- Dustin has Down syndrome. Do you think this makes him any different from other boys his age?

- Why do you think Dustin is a little shy when he goes to meet his new sister?

- Make a list of all the things Dustin does to help with Mary Ann.

Figure 6-2 *Big Brother Dustin* by A. R. Carter (1989). Cover reprinted by permission of Albert Whitman.

 Dodds, B. (1993). *My Sister Annie*. Honesdale, PA: Boyds Mills Press.

Eleven-year-old Charlie has several challenges he hopes to accomplish—joining a club called the bombers, going to a school dance, and pitching a good game for his team. An even bigger challenge is learning to accept his older sister, Annie, who has Down syndrome. It is his coach who finally helps Charlie come to terms with his sister as he explains that he also has a sibling with disabilities.

- Tell the class about Down syndrome—its characteristics, causes, etc. (some of this is included in the text).

- Coach McCarthy helps Charlie accept his sister. Tell about someone who helped you with something.

- Do you think the support group will help Charlie accept his sister? What might they talk about?

- Charlie has several challenges in his life. What are some challenges you have faced?

- What sports do you enjoy? Draw a picture of yourself participating in your favorite sport.

 Fassler, J. (1969). *One Little Girl*. New York: Behavioral Publications.

Laurie is one of the first children to touch the new snow and hear the robin chirp in the spring. But often people say that Laurie is a "slow child," and this makes her sad. Laurie's mother takes her to a special doctor who tests her and writes a letter about all the things Laurie can do as well as what she cannot do. After that, Laurie feels a lot better about herself and what she can do.

- Have students draw names out of a hat and tell, write, or draw a special message telling that student about something that he or she does well.

- Have you ever been the first one to do something? What was it?

- Laurie can jump rope 67 times in one minute. Practice jumping rope. How many times can you jump without missing?

- Laurie hears her teacher say that she is slow. This made her feel that she couldn't do anything. How might her teacher have helped her?

- Make a list of things you are good at and things you are not so good at. Share your list with a friend.

- Write a continuation of the story. Would Laurie continue to feel good about herself?

- Did anyone ever say anything about you that made you feel bad?

- If Laurie were in your class, what could you do to help her?

 Fitzgerald, J., & Fitzgerald, L. (1994). *Barnaby's Birthday*. Dallas: SRA-Macmillan/ McGraw Hill.

Written as a poem, the story tells about a birthday party for Barnaby, a little boy with Down syndrome. He opens his gifts, eats snacks, and has a cake. The reader sees that children with disabilities celebrate birthdays just like all children.

 • Encourage a discussion about birthday parties that students have had— the types of activities planned, gifts received, etc. Have students note the similarities between their parties and Barnaby's.

 • Make a "Birthdays Bulletin Board" in your classroom with the children's names and their birthdays.

• Barnaby's story is written as a poem. Write a simple poem about birthdays or parties. Illustrate your poem.

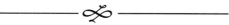

 Fleming, V. (1993). *Be Good to Eddie Lee.* New York: Philomel Books.

Christy and her friend JimBud are enjoying a spring day together looking for frog eggs when Eddie Lee, a boy with Down syndrome, joins them. JimBud isn't nice to Eddie Lee, but Christy tells him that her mother has told her, "Be good to Eddie Lee." Eddie leads Christy to a secret pond where there are frog eggs and where water lilies grow. Eddie and Christy become friends and Christy runs to tell JimBud about the discovery.

 • Explain more to the children about Down syndrome (children are born this way, they may look different but they like the same things, etc.).

• Have you ever been around someone who was being mean to another person? What did you say to stop them?

• Draw a picture of the water lilies shown in the book.

• In the beginning, JimBud calls Eddie Lee "dumb." How did Eddie Lee show that he wasn't dumb?

• At the end, Eddie Lee says that "It's what's here that counts," as he points to his heart. What did he mean by that?

• Continue the story. What do you think JimBud would say or do after Christy told him about the pond?

 Haines, S. (1995). *Becca and Sue Make Two.* Boise, ID: Writer's Press.

Becca, a six-year-old girl going into first grade, loves to go to her piano lesson on Saturday mornings. Her favorite song is "Chopsticks," especially when she plays it with her teacher. Becca enjoys learning new things. Her grandparents taught Becca a lesson one day. She learned from them that even though they did things differently than her parents, it wasn't necessarily wrong. Different people do things in different ways. The day Becca goes to first grade, she meets a friend that she likes at Buddy Study time. Her new friend's name is Sue and she has Down syndrome. Becca notices things that are different about Sue, but knows that different people do things in different ways. When Becca's teacher tells the class about a talent show they are going to have for all their parents, Becca decides she wants to play "Chopsticks" with Sue on the piano. She loves it when two people play that song! Becca's piano teacher teaches them both to play "Chopsticks" together. They work with each other on a rhyme to play the song. The talent show goes well. Becca and Sue both learn that together people do things better.

- Assign students a partner at random. In their groups of two, have them make a list of activities or things that they both like to do. Have them choose one activity on their list. After several days of the pairs trying their one activity together, have them perform their group activity before the class and tell the class what conclusions they discovered about working together.

- Becca and Sue are good friends to each other. Tell about a special friend you have.

- How could you help someone in your class who does things differently?

- What is one lesson you have learned that's important?

- With a partner, make a list of differences that you have. Then make a list of similarities. Compare the lists. Which is longer?

 Hirsch, K. (1977). *My Sister*. Minneapolis: Carolrhoda Books.

In this book, a little boy tells the story of his older sister who has mental retardation. Sometimes he is angry with her and sometimes he is embarrassed. One day when the family goes to the beach, some people are mean to her. This is when he realizes how much he loves her—just the way she is.

- Sometimes the sister makes the little boy angry because it seems like she gets the best of everything. Talk with children about feeling angry and ways to resolve their conflicts. Make a class pattern book, "I get angry when my brother / sister / friend . . . (problem), and then we . . . (solution).

- The little boy's sister has a special gift—something she is really good at. What is it?

- The boy in the story talks about the things he enjoys doing with the girl who lives next door. What do you enjoy doing with your friends?

- The sister's favorite toys are an old teddy bear and an orange dump truck. Draw a picture of one or two of your favorite toys and write about the things you do with them.

- Sometimes the brother feels that he is treated unfairly. Write about a time when you felt the same and how someone made you feel better.

- The boy's parents paint his room and add a bookcase. Design/draw a bedroom that you'd like to have.

- Sometimes the brother wishes that his sister would be like other children. If you could have one wish, what would it be?

- The children don't have names in the story. Give them names.

 Hunter, E. (1969). *Sue Ellen.* Boston: Houghton Mifflin.

This heartwarming book describes the life of Sue Ellen, an eight-year-old girl who has severe learning problems. At first, she struggles in a regular classroom; she hates school and also hates to go home since her family is very poor and her mother is sick all the time. Finally, Sue Ellen is transferred to a "special" class for children like her. Here the teacher is nice, the children care about each other, and one high school student takes a special interest in her. Life changes for Sue Ellen as she begins to learn and gains confidence and a new respect for herself.

 • With the class, make a web to describe the setting, characters, and problems that are detailed in this story.

 • Sue Ellen's class raises money for their trip and their classroom by having an auction. Using play money or chips, hold a class "auction" to "buy" things you bring in.

- If Sue Ellen were a part of your class, what are some things you could do to help her? Knowing she was tired and hungry all the time, how might the teacher have helped her?

- How do you think Sue Ellen felt when she stayed on the bus the first day going to the new school?

- Polly becomes very special to Sue Ellen. Why? Do you have a special friend?

- Write a math word problem about a class auction. Let a classmate solve the problem.

- Sue Ellen had to miss the Halloween party because she was sick. Did this ever happen to you?

 Hya-Grollman, S. (1977). *More Time to Grow: Explaining Mental Retardation to Children.* Boston: Beacon Press.

Carla is a young girl who is trying to understand the things that her younger brother Arthur does. Sometimes he ruins things and he can't ever tie his shoelaces. Carla experiences a mix of emotions, from anger to sadness, regarding her brother. The family discovers that Arthur has retardation and she becomes even more upset. Finally, she visits a friend whose daughter has also retardation and who makes her understand how special these children can be.

 - See "Questions to Think About" in the back of the book.

 - See "Activities for Children" in the back of the book.

- Carla's parents take her for a walk to talk with her about Arthur. How does your family handle a problem or a difficult situation?

- Carla and Arthur have fun singing together. Make a list of other things they could enjoy doing together.

- The illustrations are done in pencil. Sketch a portrait of someone who is special to you.

- Why do you think people are sometimes afraid of people with retardation, as the boy's dad says?

- At the end of the book, the boy talks about all the things he has learned. Write down some of the things you have learned this year. Share them with a friend.

- What are some ways you could help children with mental retardation who are in your class?

Klein, L. (1994). *Are There Stripes in Heaven?* Mahwah, NJ: Paulist Press.

Patrick is unhappy because he can't go to the video arcade with his friend because it's Sunday and time for Mass. Then it rains and he can't go outside. His older sister Colleen, who has Down syndrome, is happy, however. She meets two new friends at church and after the rain, sees a rainbow. Colleen's question, "Are there stripes in heaven?" (referring to the rainbow) prompts Patrick to appreciate even the most ordinary of moments.

 • Have the children make a list of things they are thankful for. Perhaps they could do this for several days and discuss their findings at the end of this time period.

 • Colleen likes the song, "If You're Happy and You Know It." Sing this song as a class.

• Write to the address listed for the National Down Syndrome Society in the back of the book for more information on Down syndrome.

• Draw a picture of a rainbow. Perhaps you could write a poem about rainbows.

• The girls in church acted "as though Colleen wasn't even a person." What could you say to them to make them behave differently?

 Kneeland, L. (1989). *Cookie.* Hollidaysburg, PA: Jason & Nordic Publishers.

Molly is a four-year-old girl with Down syndrome. She has difficulty communicating her needs until a special person teaches her beginning sign language. Molly then suffers fewer frustrations because she can ask for what she wants.

 • Reinforce the signs for cookie and juice shown at the end of the book. Have children practice these signs and any others you know.

 • Invite an expert to show the class additional words or phrases from American Sign Language.

 • Talk about various ways we communicate (verbal, nonverbal, etc.)

• Susan is a special friend to Molly. Tell about someone who taught you something special.

• Imagine no one could understand what you wanted or needed. Write how you might feel.

Larsen, H. (1974). *Don't Forget Tom.* **New York: Thomas Y. Crowell.**

Tom is a six-year-old boy who has mental retardation. The story explains why it takes Tom longer to learn things than others; part of his brain doesn't work properly. The story emphasizes all the things that Tom can do and helps the reader understand the challenges faced by those with developmental disabilities.

- Tom's family consists of a brother, sister, mom, and dad. Ask each child to contribute a page about his or her family to a class book or create a bulletin board about the families in your classroom.

- Using the pictures in the book that show what Tom can do, describe his actions in full sentences.

- Tell about the things that you like to do.

- Tom gets frustrated when he can't do some things that his brother and friends can do easily. Discuss what "frustrated" means and tell about a time you were frustrated.

- Tell what Tom has taught you about those with disabilities. Why will you "not forget Tom"?

 Little, J. (1968). *Take Wing.* **Boston: Little, Brown.**

Laurel takes good care of her younger brother James, who appears to be slower and more unsure of himself than other boys at the age of seven. Laurel's parents do not directly recognize that Laurel isn't making friends of her own. Finally, a girl named Barbara befriends Laurel, but quickly withdraws due to a secret of her own. At the end of the story, we find that Barbara has a big sister, Alice, who has severe mental retardation.

- James seems to be slower than other boys his age. Talk about individual differences. How old were the children when they learned to ride a bike? jump rope? do a sleepover with a friend?

- Barbara was hesitant to tell Laurel about Alice. Why do you think so?

- Have you ever had a secret? Did you tell your secret?

- Laurel is a good sister to James. Write a description of a good brother, sister, or friend.

- What can both Laurel and Barbara do to help their siblings?
- Research mental retardation to find out more about it.

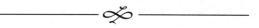

 McNey, M., with ARC of Hennepin County. (1996). *Leslie's Story: A Book About a Girl with Mental Retardation.* **Minneapolis: Lerner Publications.**

Told in the first person and through descriptive black and white photographs, this is the story of Leslie Fish. She is a twelve-year-old whose brain was damaged as a result of meningitis. She refers to herself as "handicapped" because she doesn't like the term "mental retardation." Leslie also wears hearing aids because the meningitis caused some hearing loss. Her story focuses on her family and school activities. Skiing and ice skating are especially important to her since she lives in Minnesota. Leslie skates with her Special Olympics team at the National Figure Skating Championships. Her story concludes with the celebration of her bat mitzvah. The book also includes "Information about Mental Retardation" and a glossary.

 • Leslie's brain was damaged as a result of having meningitis when she was a baby. Ask students to talk with their parents about illnesses they had during infancy or when they were toddlers. A pediatrician could also be invited to talk with students about childhood illnesses including meningitis.

 • Leslie likes to skate fast and helps children who have trouble skating. Arrange a field trip to a skating rink with instruction for students who don't skate.

 • Leslie participates in Special Olympics. Write to the Special Olympics organization for information to share with students.

 • Leslie talks about her bat mitzvah. Gather more information about this ceremony to share with students. A field trip or guest speaker may also be helpful.

- Leslie tells about activities that she enjoys with her mom, dad, and brother. Divide large drawing paper into sections—one for each member of your family. Draw and write about an activity that you enjoy doing with each.

 Ominsky, E. (1977). *Jon O.: A Special Boy.* **Englewood Cliffs, NJ: Prentice Hall.**

Jon O. is a little boy who has Down syndrome. Although it takes him longer than others to learn things, he does learn things at his own pace. The story focuses on the things that Jon O. can do well and the fact that he helps his friends as much as his friends help him.

- Jon O. is very helpful around the house. As a class, make a list of all the jobs the children do at home. Make a semantic map of all the jobs by grouping them into categories.

- Jon O. enjoys hiking with his brothers and watching television after school. Draw and label a picture of your favorite after school activities. Add your picture to the "After School Activities" bulletin board.

- Look up Down syndrome in the encyclopedia or on the internet to find out more about it.

- Think about some reasons why Jon O. is special.

- It took a long time for Jon O. to walk and talk. Find out how old you were when you took your first steps and spoke your first words. Do a survey of ten friends. Make a bar graph showing the results of your survey.

- Jon O. had trouble remembering his colors and numbers. What has been difficult for you to remember? How did you finally do it?

- Jon O. helps the members of his family and they help him. Make a list of things that you do to help the people in your family.

 O'Shaughnessy, E. (1992). *Somebody Called Me a Retard Today . . . and My Heart Felt Sad.* New York: Walker.

Written in simple text and illustrated with watercolors, this book is the story of a young girl with mental retardation. Her thoughts and reactions when someone calls her a "retard" make the reader aware of the feelings of those who may be different in some way. The reader is challenged to look at the strengths of others rather than the weaknesses.

- Plan an activity where all the children in the class write one positive thing about each person. Compile all the responses and give them to each individual.

- Someone makes the girl in the story feel bad by calling her a name. Have you ever had a similar experience? How did you feel?

- The girl in the story can do many things well. What are some things that you do well? Draw a picture of yourself doing one of these things. Write a sentence under the picture to describe it.

- The girl's father appears to be an important person in her life. Tell about an important person in your life.

- Write a letter to the girl in this story to make her feel better.

 Rheingrover, J. S. (1996). *Veronica's First Year*. Morton Grove, IL: Albert Whitman.

Nathan waited a long time for his baby sister to be born. When she was born, her grandmother said she was a "special baby." Nathan soon finds out that she has Down syndrome and he wonders what that means. Nathan looks through his own baby photo album, and promises that he will help Veronica. During Veronica's first year, the family fills Veronica's album. Nathan has one special picture in the album that he likes best.

- Invite a physician to explain more about Down syndrome.

- Bring in pictures from your first year. Share them with the class and tell which one is your favorite and why.

- If you have a baby brother or sister, tell what happened when he or she was born.

- How can Nathan help Veronica learn new things?

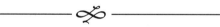

 Rabe, B. (1988). *Where's Chimpy?* Morton Grove, IL: Albert Whitman.

Misty, a little girl with Down syndrome, discovers that she has misplaced her stuffed toy monkey and sleeping buddy, Chimpy. Her dad helps her rethink her day until she remembers where she last put Chimpy and happily takes him to bed with her. The photographs clearly depict a wonderful father-daughter relationship.

- Create a "Found Box" in your classroom where children can put items they find in the classroom that are not theirs.

- Tell or write about a time when you lost something and how you went about looking for it.

- Write a lost and found ad in search of something special that you lost.

- Misty enjoys reading stories with her dad. Draw or write about what you like to do with your dad or someone special.

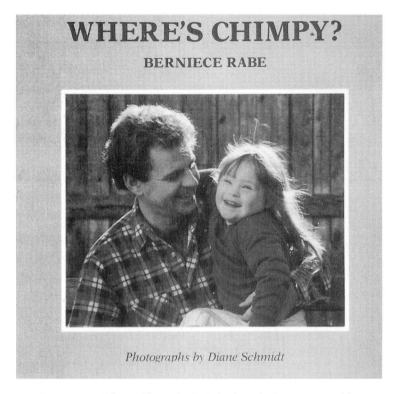

WHERE'S CHIMPY?

BERNIECE RABE

Photographs by Diane Schmidt

Figure 6-3 *Where's Chimpy* by B. Rabe (1988). Cover reprinted by permission of Albert Whitman.

 Sobol, H. L. (1977). *My Brother Steven Is Retarded.* **New York: Macmillan.**

This story revolves around eleven-year-old Beth and her relationship with her older brother Steven, who has mental retardation. Written in the first person, it is a candid account of the true feelings—positive and negative— experienced by Beth with regard to Steven. These feelings range from embarrassment, to pride, to concern for Steven's future. Photographs clearly depict the highs and lows of this sibling relationship.

 • Ask students to draw a picture of their families. They could tell or write about their pictures and then display them on a "Families" bulletin board.

• Sometimes Beth is upset with Steven and sometimes she is happy. If you have a brother or sister, tell about a time you were happy or upset with him or her.

- Beth and Steven have a dog named Smokey. If you have a pet, tell about it.

- Beth and her father like to walk their dog Smokey together. What do you like to do with a parent or friend in your spare time?

- Write an acrostic poem using the word *brother* or *sister*. (See format in Appendix A.)

- Write a letter to your brother, sister, or a special friend telling them how important he or she is to you.

 Thompson, M. (1992). *My Brother Matthew*. Kensington, MD: Woodbine House.

This is the story of two brothers named David and Matthew. David tells the story of when Matthew was born and had to stay in the hospital. When he came home, he had a special therapy program because he had disabilities. In

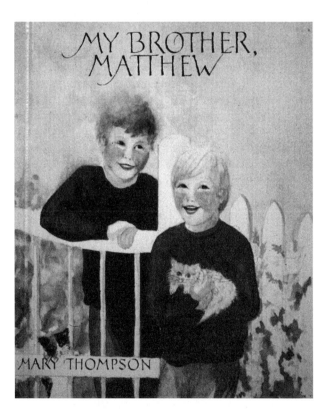

Figure 6-4 *My Brother Matthew* by M. Thompson (1992). Cover reprinted by permission of Woodbine House.

spite of the problems, David and Matthew become close brothers who have their own special way of communicating.

- Talk about why some babies can't come home from the hospital right away with their mothers—low birth weight, jaundice, etc. Invite a neonatal nurse in to talk with children about some of the new medical developments for infants.

- Tell about your brother or sister or a friend with whom you are close. What kinds of things do you enjoy doing together?

- Matthew likes cats a lot. Do you have a pet or favorite animal? Draw a picture of it.

- How do you think David felt when his mother had to spend a lot of time with Matthew?

- Continue this story by predicting what David or Matthew will do next.

Students can work together to write a story.

Testa, M. (1994). *Thumbs Up, Rico!* **Morton Grove, IL: Albert Whitman.**

Rico is a little boy who has Down syndrome. This book contains three short stories that feature Rico and different aspects of his life. In the first, Rico is teased by, but finally befriends, a boy named Caesar. In the second, he has a conflict with his sister Nina over whether she will go to his basketball game or to a party. In the third, Rico has trouble drawing for art class, but finally draws a picture of himself playing basketball. Rico's love of basketball and the success he finds through his courage are themes that run through all three stories,.

 • Invite a health practitioner to tell the class more about Down syndrome.

• Rico loves basketball. Do you play a sport? What is it?

• Draw a picture of yourself playing your favorite sport.

• Rico has a hard time in art class. What is your favorite and least favorite subject in school?

• Nina is special to Rico. Write about a special brother, sister, or friend that you have.

• Why is the name of the book *Thumbs Up, Rico!*?

 Wright, B. R. (1981). *My Sister is Different.* **Milwaukee: Raintree Children's Books.**

This book portrays what life is like for Carlo, a little boy whose older sister, Terry, has mental retardation. Carlo resents Terry because he has a lot of responsibility for her. One day, he loses Terry in a store and realizes how special she is to him and to others around her. Carlo discovers that he loves his sister very much.

 • Carlo says that his sister is "different." Talk about the ways that students are different from each other.

 • Carlo thinks that Terry is lost in the store. Talk with children about what they should do if they ever get lost in a store or mall.

• Carlo is sometimes embarrassed by his sister. Write about a time when you were embarrassed.

• What special abilities does Terry have?

- Carlo's grandmother said he has a "dried up" heart. What did she mean by that?

- Carlo took Terry Christmas shopping. Make coupons for things that you could give or do for the people in your family.

- Terry was excited that she got to find the bathroom all by herself in the store. Tell or write about the first time you got to do something by yourself. Is there something that you're looking forward to doing that will make you feel grown-up?

- Terry gives Carlo a special birthday card, and Carlo makes Terry a special card at the end of the story. Make a card for someone you love and tell how special he or she is.

- Grandma and Carlo talk about his heart. Cut out large paper hearts and decorate them to show Carlo's heart at the end of the story.

CHAPTER 7

LITERATURE ABOUT CHILDREN WITH VISUAL IMPAIRMENT

The Individuals with Disabilities Education Act (IDEA) uses the term "visual impairment" as an umbrella term that includes partial sightedness and total blindness. IDEA says it is an impairment in vision that, even with correction, adversely affects a child's educational performance. There are three types of visual impairment: 1) those who are functionally blind use Braille but have vision for environmental tasks, 2) those who have low vision can read with magnification, and 3) those who are totally blind must use tactual and auditory learning: they receive no meaningful input through vision (Turnbull, Turnbull, Shank, & Leal, 1995).

According to the Nineteenth Annual Report to Congress on the Implementation of the Individuals with Disabilities Education Act (1997), approximately 25,484 children between the ages of six and twenty-one are identified as having a visual impairment—one percent of the total number of children with disabilities.

Though some students with visual impairments receive educational services in residential schools, many are in the general education classroom. According to Turnbull et al. (1995), forty-two percent of students are in such classes for at least eighty percent of the school day. Implications for the professional are vast. Many students with visual impairments face an inability to learn incidentally from the environment. Therefore, "students who are visually impaired not only require instruction in academic areas but also in skills needed to compensate for their loss of vision" (Hunt & Marshall, 1994, p. 411). Four types of curricula are essential for students with visual impairment: 1) general curriculum with adaptations, 2) skills learned incidentally by others, 3) skills to access academic curriculum, and 4) disability-specific skills (Turnbull et al., 1995).

First, general education teachers may utilize the general curriculum for those with disabilities, but make adaptations such as giving extra support, using larger print, or incorporating braille. Braille can be produced on a Braillewriter or on a hand-held slate with a stylus. It can also be produced by a computer with a braille printer.

Skills that are learned incidentally by others must be taught directly to some students with visual impairments. These skills include orientation and mobility. The goal of orientation and mobility training is "to enable the student to enter any environment, familiar or unfamiliar, and to function safely, efficiently, gracefully, and independently" (Hill & Ponder, 1976, p. 1). Orientation and mobility systems include the sighted cane, cane travel, guide dog, and electronic travel aids.

Skills to access the academic curriculum include training in specialized study skills and the use of adaptive equipment. Available assistive technology includes closed circuit television (which enlarges print size on the television screen), voice output for computers, and the Optacon (which converts print to tactile output), among others (Hunt & Marshall, 1994). Finally, students may need to be taught directly in disability-specific skills, such as self-advocacy and health/eye care.

The literature selections depict children of varying ages with visual impairments. The reader becomes aware of their daily struggles and triumphs, and acquires incidental information about assistive devices and methods used to compensate for the loss of vision.

REFERENCES

Hill, E., & Ponder, P. (1976). *Orientation and mobility techniques.* New York: American Foundation for the Blind.

Hunt, N., and Marshall, K. (1994). *Exceptional children and youth.* Boston: Houghton Mifflin.

Turnbull, A. P., Turnbull, H. R., Shank, M., & Leal, D. (1995). *Exceptional lives: Special education in today's schools.* Englewood Cliffs, NJ: Prentice Hall.

U.S. Department of Education (1997). Nineteenth annual report to Congress on the implementation of the Individuals with Disabilities Education Act. Washington, DC: U.S. Government Printing Office.

LITERATURE SELECTIONS

 Aiello, B., & Shulman, J. (1988). *Business Is Looking Up.* Frederick, MD: Twenty-first Century Books.

Renaldo, the main character of this book, is blind. This story portrays Renaldo's adventure with business. It shows the main character in a very positive light.

The story shows how children with disabilities can do everyday normal things. There is also a description of Renaldo at the beginning that includes his likes and dislikes. This makes it easy for a child to relate to the main character. There are also very helpful questions and answers in the back of the book typical of those that might be asked by children in elementary school.

 • Have children bring in several birthday cards or other greeting cards that they've received. Have them share the cards and then design one for a friend.

• Renaldo and his brother like to play Scrabble after dinner. In small groups, play Scrabble during "free time."

• Jeremy made a card to tell his stepmother that "he liked having her around." Make a card for someone special to you.

• Explain the following terms: investment, marketing research, advertising.

• Design a birthday card for your teacher, principal, pen pal, President of the United States, etc.

• Renaldo refers to his mom as "the expert" as he seeks her advice. Whose opinions do you value?

• Renaldo and Jinx's card business becomes too successful. How would you have solved their problem?

• There are "Questions for Renaldo" at the end of the book. The answers provide lots of information. Is there something that you'd like to ask Renaldo?

• Do you think Renaldo's idea for "R.R. & J.B. Stepcards" is a good one?

• Design a greeting card using a computer software program.

• Write to the organization on p. 35 for a catalog of books on tape.

• Since Renaldo is blind, his mother helps him find his food by pretending his plate is like a clock. Try to put food on your plate according to a clock pattern. Do you think this would help Renaldo?

 Bergman, T. (1989). *Seeing in Special Ways: Children Living with Blindness.* **Milwaukee: Gareth Stevens.**

In this delightful and informative book, the author talks with a number of children who are either blind or have partial sight. They share their hopes, dreams, fears, and thoughts about blindness, living in a residential school, and coping in a sightless world.

• Andrew uses a cane. Invite a vision specialist to come and explain the different types of walking canes. Blindfolded, try to use one.

 • Obtain a descriptive video and show it to the class. These can be found at most libraries in a special services division.

 • Make a "Feel It" box (a covered shoe box with a hole in one end). Put some items in the box. Ask children to try to guess what is in the box without seeing it.

• In the back of the book are questions from children about blindness. Are there other questions you would ask some of the children in this book?

• Try to learn the braille symbols for a few words. Share your words with a friend; let him or her guess what the words are.

Figure 7-1   *Seeing in Special Ways* by T. Bergman (1989). Cover reprinted by permission of Gareth Stevens Publishers.

- Write to one of the organizations in the back of the book for more information.

- Try to spend fifteen minutes in your home blindfolded. What special problems did you encounter? (Make sure you have someone to keep you safe when you do this.)

 Brown, M. (1979). *Arthur's Eyes.* **Boston: Little, Brown.**

Arthur is having a terrible time seeing. He can't see the board in school and he misses all the baskets in gym. Finally, Arthur gets glasses, but he is teased so terribly he hides them. Now things are worse than ever. When the principal tells Arthur that he has to wear glasses to read, Arthur feels better and decides to wear his glasses. Now even Francine, who had teased him before, wants to wear glasses.

 • An optometrist determined that Arthur needed glasses. Ask the school nurse or an optometrist to test the children's vision.

 • Arrange for the class to visit an optical shop. Try on various frames.

- Do a vision survey of teachers and staff in your school. Gather data concerning the use of glasses. Display information showing the number of people who wear glasses all the time, sometimes, and never in a bar graph. What conclusions can you draw?

- How does Arthur feel about his glasses?

- Arthur was embarrassed when he went into the wrong bathroom. Tell about a time when you were embarrassed.

- Write what Arthur's classmates should have said to him when he got his glasses.

- Arthur's friends laughed at him when he wore glasses. Has anyone ever made fun of you? Write about a good way to handle the situation.

- Did you ever try to hide something from someone or to keep a secret? Tell or write your story including how you were found out.

- Francine wears her "movie star glasses" to make her concentrate and feel more beautiful. Draw and write about one of your treasures that makes you feel special.

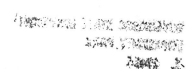

Cohen, M. (1983). *See You Tomorrow, Charles.* **New York: Greenwillow Books.**

Charles is a new boy in class and he is blind. His classmates feel awkward around him and aren't quite sure of what to say or do. One day while at recess, several of the children, including Charles, venture through a large door into the basement of the school where it is very dark. Charles feels his way around until he finds the door knob and gets the children out. The children realize that Charles is their peer, and that there are things that he can do even better than they can.

 • The children work with clay. Have students wear a blindfold and create something made of modeling clay or Play-Doh.

 • Charles can play checkers even though he's blind. How is he able to do that? Have students work in small groups to adapt a checkers game or another game so that a child who is blind could play.

• Close your eyes for five minutes and try to make your way around your house. What problems did you experience?

• Charles is learning to read braille. Research braille and how it is used by the blind to read.

• Charles uses his hands to accomplish many things. What are some things that he uses his hands for?

• Danny seems to have some inappropriate behavior. List the things he says or does that should be changed. What should Danny say or do instead?

• The teacher has a discussion with the children about real and imaginary characters. Make lists that identify real and imaginary characters from television programs and movies that children have seen and from books that they've read.

• The teacher thinks that Charles can find his own seat in the classroom. Have students take turns wearing a blindfold, finding their seats in the classroom, or finding another location in the school with a student escort.

• Charles becomes a hero at the end of the story. Write a similar story of a hero or heroine with a disability.

———————— ✂ ————————

Condra, E. (1994). *See the Ocean.* Nashville, TN: Ideals Children's Books.

Nellie loves going to the ocean every year with her parents and two brothers. Each time they go, the boys compete to see who can see the ocean first. Nellie never competes—until this year. This year, there is a heavy mist that makes the ocean hard to see. Nellie, however, can "see with her mind." It is not until the end of the book that the reader learns that Nellie is blind. The story, accompanied by lovely oil paintings, is an American Bestseller "Pick of the Lists."

- Collect data about the children's favorite places to visit. Display these on a bar graph.

- Write about your trip to the beach or another place you enjoy.

- Nellie compares the ocean to an old man. Write a description of something where you compare it to something else.

- Nellie enjoys the sounds she hears at the beach. Close your eyes and listen. What sounds do you hear?

- How could you help a classmate who is blind or visually impaired?

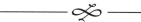

 Eyerly, J. (1981). *The Seeing Summer.* New York: J. B. Lippincott.

Carey is a ten-year-old girl who wishes desperately for a new best friend to replace her neighbor who moved away. When she hears the news that a new family with a girl her age is moving in next door she is ecstatic, until she finds out that her new neighbor, Jenny, is blind and walks with a cane. Carey is crushed that she will not have a friend who can do everything that she does. To her surprise, Jenny is perfectly capable of doing many of the things Carey likes to do, such as cooking, playing cards, climbing trees, and reading her own books. When Carey leaves Jenny alone on a bench for fifteen minutes, she is kidnapped by two strangers and held for ransom. Carey carefully begins collecting clues and eventually tracks down the kidnappers and is captured and held with Jenny. Together the girls stay calm and eventually discover a way to escape from their terrifying situation and return home better friends than ever.

- Plan a scavenger hunt with written clues to the treasures.

- The girls are kidnapped. Talk about the dangers of strangers and possible responses. A community program may be available to provide this information.

- Jenny is blind and walks with a cane. In pairs, blindfold one person and try to walk around using a large stick. Reverse roles and let the other person try. What problems did you encounter?

- Have any of your best friends ever moved away? How did you feel?

- Write about some of the things you like to do with your friends. Draw a picture to accompany your story.

- Using a simple picture book, write a "descriptive story" that tells a blind child about the illustrations as well as the story.

- Jenny and Carey have a scary experience together and solve their problem successfully. How else might they have solved the problem?

 Hermann, H., & Hermann, B. (1988). *Jenny's Magic Wand.* **New York: Franklin Watts.**

In preparation for inclusion in a regular education classroom, Jenny attends a special school where she learns strategies that help her. She thinks of her cane as a magic wand because it can lead her "through the world" and she can go places that she could not go before. The black and white photographs show the many activities that ultimately contribute to her success.

 • Borrow a cane or let students simply use a yard/meter stick to maneuver around the classroom and/or playground while blindfolded. Be sure to have children take a partner with them.

- Jenny attended a special school to prepare her for a regular school. Make a list of things you do during the summer to prepare for the start of the school year.

- Jenny refers to her cane as a magic wand. If you could have something magical, what would it be? Write a story about yourself and your special power.

- The children enjoy learning to make lunch. Try to make a peanut butter and jelly sandwich while you're blindfolded.

- Ms. Taylor asked the children to tell about funny things they remember. Tell about something that you remember doing that was funny.

- Jenny finds the keys for her teacher because she had listened to where Mrs. Wade "fiddled" with them. Why do you think the other children treated her differently then?

- Does Jenny want to be treated differently from the others? Why?

Litchfield, A. B. (1977). *A Cane in Her Hand*. Morton Grove, IL: Albert Whitman.

In this book, Val tells her own story of how she came to use a long cane. She has always worn glasses, but eventually has a hard time seeing even with glasses. A special teacher at school helps her with her schoolwork and teaches her to use the cane. At first Val doesn't like it because she's afraid her friends won't understand. She is soon relieved and happy when they not only understand, but want to learn to use it too.

 • Val's ophthalmologist tested her eyes. Invite an ophthalmologist to class to talk about care of the eyes.

 • Invite an optometrist to class to talk about how glasses help people see.

 • Ask the physical education teacher to set up an obstacle course in the gym or outdoors. Have students try it sighted and then blindfolded with the help of a long stick.

 • Invite a pediatric ophthalmologist to speak about various visual impairments and their treatments.

 • Given common items in a "Feel Box", have students identify the items by only using their sense of touch.

• Blindfolded, practice walking around the room using a stick to help you to "see."

• Keeping your hand high, walk around the school playground. Then try it blindfolded with the help of a long stick.

• After her doctor's appointment, Valerie's family goes out to eat. She can't enjoy her cheeseburger because she's so worried about her eyes. Write about a time when you were really worried about something.

 Martin, B. & Archembault, J. (1987). *Knots on a Counting Rope*. New York: Henry Holt.

Grandfather and Boy alternate telling the story of Boy's birth, growing, and dealing with his blindness. They talk about the many ways to see and recall how Boy learned to ride his horse and see with his heart. Each time the story is told, Grandfather adds a knot to the counting rope, marking the passage of time. This Native American story is beautifully illustrated and the conversational style of the text brings the reader into the story.

• Students could use a 4x6 card with their school picture to illustrate the history and meaning of their names. It could make for an interesting bulletin board.

 • Students could tell about special events that have taken place in the classroom. A knot could be added to a class counting rope.

• Grandfather and Boy tell the story of Boy's birth. Talk with your parents about your birth or arrival (adoption). Record the story in writing, illustrations, or on tape.

• Grandfather and Boy tell how Boy was named. Find out how you were named and what your name means.

• Boy describes the color blue: "Blue is the morning . . . the sunrise . . . the sky . . ." Choose a color. Write a poem describing it or make a book telling about and illustrating the color you have chosen.

• Grandfather and Boy have a wonderful conversation. If you could talk with anyone, who would it be? What would you like to talk about? Write some of your conversation.

 McMahon, P. (1995). *Listen for the Bus—David's Story*. Honesdale, PA: Boyd Mills Press.

Through detailed photographs and descriptive text the author tells the story of a typical school day in David's life. David is a kindergartner who is blind and hearing impaired. David is portrayed as a typical little boy as he is included in a regular kindergarten and participates in after-school activities. The book shows the special relationships between David and his parents.

 • Talk about some of the problems that David might have during the school day. His teacher uses "knobby" paper so David knows where his cubby is. Brainstorm a list of some other things that could be done to help David at school.

 • Each child in the story has made a list of his or her favorite things. Ask children to make a list of their favorite things and display the lists with their photographs as David's class did.

• David has a special list of things he likes to do. Write a list of things that you like to do.

• Close your eyes and like David, feel different rocks. What are some words that describe these rocks?

- If you ride a bus to school, listen to the noises it makes. Write a descriptive paragraph called "Listen to the Bus."

- Blindfolded, try to get around the classroom for a short period of time. What are some problems you encountered?

- Go out to the school playground. After putting on a blindfold, listen to the sounds around you for ten minutes. Make a list of everything you heard.

- David brought a special rock to school. Bring one of your treasures to school. Ask three friends to feel your treasure as they are blindfolded, guess what the object is, and then write a short description of it.

- David enjoys working with clay. Create a clay or Play-Doh project.

- David enjoys doing special things with his mom and dad. Make a Venn diagram showing what you enjoy doing with each of your parents separately and together.

- *Listen for the Bus* tells of a day in David's life. Write a story of one of your favorite school days. Edit and then "publish" it in book form.

Rider-Montgomery, Elizabeth. (1979). *"Seeing" in the Dark*. Champaign, IL: Garrard Publishing.

Kay is a new girl at school and she is blind. Because she had such bad experiences at her old school, she is dreading this one. At first, the students do not believe she is blind and they tease her. When they realize that she is telling the truth, they begin to play with her. Kay truly wins their friendship when she safely leads them out of the building during a school fire.

 • Invite someone to demonstrate a Braille writer and to show braille and large print books.

 • Do the simulation that Mr. Grun's class did with the blindfolds. Write a class story about the experience.

• Kay felt very alone at her old school. Write about a time when you felt very alone.

• Miss Stone is a special friend to Kay. Describe one of your special friends.

• Make "glasses" out of cardboard (frames) and wax paper (lenses). Tie them in the back with string. What might it have been like to be lost in the smoky school?

• Why do the children tease Kay?

• Sometimes most children don't feel like going to school. If you could have a day off, what would you do? Write an itinerary for your day.

• The children were mean to Kay during recess. Pretend that you were there. Write about your role in the situation.

 Sargent, S., & Wirt, D. A. (1983). *My Favorite Place*. Nashville, TN: Abrington Press.

The little girl in this story tells of her trip to the beach with her family. She describes the things she hears, the salty ocean air she smells, and the sun's warm rays she feels. These are things she likes. It is not until the end of the story that the reader knows that the girl cannot see. This does not stop her from enjoying her favorite place to be—the ocean.

 • Plan a tasting experience. Blindfolded, have students try to identify various foods presented to them to taste. Is it hard to identify these things without seeing them?

• Repeat the preceding activity, but this time have students try to identify items by feeling them.

 • Repeat the first activity, but this time have students try to identify items by smelling them.

• Close your eyes for a few minutes and concentrate on all the things around you that you can hear, smell, touch, or taste. Discuss your experience with a friend.

• Make a collage of the "five senses" including magazine pictures of things you can see, hear, touch, taste, or smell.

 Thomas, W. E. (1980). *The New Boy Is Blind.* New York: Julien Messner.

Ricky is a new boy at school who has special accommodations in the general education classroom for his blindness. For example, he uses a "Brailler" to do his work, which is translated by a special teacher. He also uses sandpaper letters to learn the alphabet. Unlike the other students in his class, he goes home for lunch because of his problems with mobility. Eventually, Ricky and his classmates receive the mobility training needed to make Ricky's time in school easier.

 • Obtain a "brailler" and demonstrate it to the class. Let everyone try using it.

 • Ricky used sandpaper letters. Obtain a set of sandpaper letters from a Montessori school. Ask children to close their eyes to trace a letter, guess what it is, and then see if they were right.

• Ricky's mom is concerned about him at school. Tell or write about a time when one of your parents was worried about you.

• Mr. Allen had difficulty explaining the word "blue" to Ricky. Choose a color to explain. Write and illustrate a poem, for example, "Blue is . . ."

• Ricky's classmates offered him lots of help. What would you ask to do for Ricky?

• Play "I Spy" or 20 Questions.

• Mr. Norman, a "trainer" from the Blind Institute, created a raised diagram of the classroom so that Ricky could get around better. Make a diagram of your classroom using glue or yarn glued to cardboard so that you'll be able to feel the layout. Try maneuvering around the classroom with your eyes closed.

- Working with a partner, take turns guiding each other walking, as Ricky was helped (pp. 34–36).

- Ricky learned to do various activities on the playground. Try some of them with your eyes closed.

- Plan a day at your home if Ricky could visit.

- The children were looking forward to going to an amusement park. Describe your favorite ride so that Ricky will understand what it is like.

 Whelan, G. (1991). *Hannah.* **New York: Alfred A. Knopf.**

This story is set in 1887 in northern Michigan. Miss Robbin, a teacher, becomes Hannah's saving grace as she comes to live with Hannah's family and is an advocate for Hannah. In particular, Miss Robbin wants Hannah to be able to go to school. After some debate, Hannah goes to school where she loves to learn and makes friends. In the end, her friends help her earn the money for a stylus that will help her write in braille.

 • Miss Robbin makes an abacus for Hannah. She explains that "this is the way people counted two thousand years ago." Gather information about the history of the abacus and teach children how to use one.

 • View the movie, "The Miracle Worker." Compare and contrast Hannah's situation with that of Helen Keller.

 • Miss Robbin teaches Hannah to pour her milk. Invite students to try the same method using a pitcher of water.

- Hannah wonders what the new teacher will be like. Describe your teacher, a parent, or someone else special to you by comparing him or her to concrete objects as Hannah does at the beginning of the story.

- Make a list of the advantages and disadvantages of having a teacher live with you or in your neighborhood.

- This story takes place in northern Michigan in 1887. Research information about this setting.

- Miss Robbin tells Hannah ". . . you see some things people with perfectly good eyes don't." What did Miss Robbin mean?

- Miss Robbin is very complimentary of Mrs. Thomas's cooking. Write a note to the cook in your family or to the school lunch staff thanking them for a delicious meal. Use interesting and descriptive words.

- Write an essay about Hannah's mother. How did she change during the story and why?

- Miss Robbin teaches Hannah how to get around the farm using her sense of touch. Think about your own house. What items, if felt, could indicate what room you were in?

- Why do you think Hannah's mother doesn't want her to go to school?

- Compare ways of life (for example, cooking, clothing) today with those of the past as shown in this book. Write about or draw examples of differences.

- Hannah's friends helped her with the money to buy the stylus. Tell or write about a time when your friends helped you or you helped a friend.

 Wosmek, F. (1976). *A Bowl of Sun*. Morton Grove, IL: Children's Press.

This is a delightful story of a blind girl, Megan, who lives with her father, Mike, in a house by the sea. For years, Megan helps her father in his store as he makes leather sandals. Finally, Mike decides that they must move to Boston to be close to a school for the blind. Megan is much more dependent in this new environment and wishes things were the same as they were in the house by the sea. However, with the help of a new friend, Rose, Megan adjusts and even learns how to use a potter's wheel. As she gives her father a carefully made clay bowl, she vows that when she finishes school, they will someday be partners in a business by the sea.

 • Megan is going to learn braille at her new school. Invite a resource person in to offer the children an opportunity to learn a few braille configurations.

- Blindfolded, try to make a clay figure like Megan did.

- How do you think Megan was able to do so much in her house by the sea when she was unable to see?

- Why was Megan afraid to have a party? Why did her father want her to have one?

- Mike and Megan like to spend time at the beach together. Where do you like to spend time with a friend?

 Yolen, J. (1977). *The Seeing Stick*. New York: Thomas Y. Crowell.

This is the story of Huei Ming, a girl who is blind, and her emperor father who is sad for his daughter, but cannot cry for her because of his position as emperor of Peking. He offers a reward of jewels for anyone who can help his daughter. Many people try, but fail. One day an old man comes to the city with his "stick that sees," and after touching the faces of the guards, cuts their portraits into the wood of the stick. They lead him into the palace where the princess is taught to "see" by feeling things and feeling the carvings on the stick. Now that his daughter can "see," her father cries and rewards the man, and allows him to stay in the city with them. It is not until the end of the story that the reader finds out that the old man is also blind.

 - The story is a classic folk tale. Share some other folk tales with students. They could respond to the tales through art, music, or writing.

 - Ask students to research the meaning of their names and share the information with the class. This could be an interesting bulletin board.

- In the back of the book is information about Huei Ming's name. It is a poetic name given by her parents for the "blind princess," a darkened moon, with the hope of becoming bright and full in the future. Did this wish come true?

- Close your eyes and feel something, with the purpose of drawing it from "seeing" it with your fingers.

- Why do you suppose the emperor cried at the end of the story?

- What can the story teach us about those who are blind?

CHAPTER 8

LITERATURE ABOUT CHILDREN WITH LEARNING DISABILITIES

There has been some debate about the definition of learning disabilities. Nationally, two definitions are used most often. First is the federal government's definition as included in the Individuals with Disabilities Education Act (IDEA) (cited in Smith & Luckasson, 1992):

> "Specific learning disability" means a disorder in one or more of the basic psychological processes involved in understanding or in using language, spoken or written, which may manifest itself in an imperfect ability to listen, think, speak, read, write or do mathematical calculations. The term includes such conditions as perceptual handicaps, brain injury, minimal brain dysfunction, dyslexia and developmental aphasia. The term does not include children who have learning problems which are primarily the result of visual, hearing, or motor handicaps, of mental retardation, of emotional disturbance, or of environmental, cultural or economic disadvantage.

A second, more recent definition, was proposed by the National Joint Committee on Learning Disabilities (cited in Smith & Luckasson, 1992):

> Learning disabilities is a general term that refers to a heterogeneous group of disorders manifested by significant difficulties in the acquisition and use of listening, speaking, reading, writing, reasoning, or mathematical abilities. These disorders are intrinsic to the individual, presumed to be due to central nervous system dysfunction, and may occur across the life span. Problems in self-regulatory behaviors, social perception, and social interaction may exist with learning disabilities but do not by themselves constitute a learning disability. Although learning disabilities may occur concomitantly with other handicapping conditions (for example, sensory impairment, mental retardation, serious emotional disturbance) or with extrinsic influences (such as cultural differences or insufficient or inappropriate instruction), they are not the result of those conditions or influences.

The difference between these definitions basically rests in the orientation about the causes of the disability (Smith & Luckasson, 1992). Either definition may be used by individual states as the basis for their varying criteria for identification. Most states use formulas combining factors such as a student's age, intelligence quotient, achievement test results, and other performance data (Forness, Sinclair, & Guthrie, 1983). In general, these factors are used to identify a discrepancy between ability and achievement in one or more areas.

According to the Nineteenth Annual Report to Congress on the Implementation of the Individuals with Disabilities Education Act (1997), approximately 2,597,231 children between the ages of six and twenty-one are identified as having a learning disability—fifty-one percent of the total number of children with disabilities. Because of different definitions of learning disabilities used by states, educational service options will vary. However, in many cases, students with learning disabilities are served in some capacity in the general education classroom.

There are many different types of learning disabilities. Some examples are: 1) dyslexia, which indicates a severe reading disorder; 2) dysgraphia, which indicates a writing disorder; and 3) dyscalculia, which indicates a problem in mathematics. Each of these types of learning disabilities is very complex and warrants some explanation, although it is admittedly limited due to the overall purposes of this text. For those with *dyslexia*, word knowledge and word recognition cause difficulty for myriad reasons. Sometimes the visual or auditory memory is weak, interrupting the retrieval of words or the grapheme/phoneme associations that are a part of recognition. Sometimes students cannot use context to either pronounce or determine the meaning of unknown words. In addition, comprehension may be impaired because students cannot adequately relate new information to prior knowledge or cannot use the organization of important ideas in text material. For those with *dysgraphia*, handwriting may be difficult due to slow writing, spacing problems, and/or poor formation of letters. In addition, they may display immature composition. Those with *dyscalculia* may experience problems understanding the "language" of math and/or problems in spatial areas that affect their math performance.

Teachers of students with learning disabilities must be aware of curricular and instructional modifications that best meet the individual learning needs of the child. In addition, teachers must be adept at behavior management, since many children display behavioral or other problems in addition to academic problems. For example, from thirty to sixty percent of children with Attention Deficit Disorders (ADD) have learning disabilities (see Chapter 5 for additional information on ADHD/ADD).

The literature selections depict children with a variety of learning disabilities. In spite of their academic challenges, many have exemplary skills in other areas. Readers become more aware of the nature of learning disabilities, as well as ways these children compensate in the classroom.

REFERENCES

Forness, S. R., Sinclair, E., & Guthrie, D. (1983). Learning disability discrepancy formulas: Their use in actual practice. *Learning Disability Quarterly*, 6, 107–114.

National Joint Committee on Learning Disabilities. (1988). (Letter to NJCLD member organizations).

Smith, D., & Luckasson, R. (1992). *Introduction to special education: Teaching in an age of challenge*. Boston: Allyn & Bacon.

U.S. Department of Education (1997). Nineteenth annual report to Congress on the implementation of the Individuals with Disabilities Education Act. Washington, DC: U.S. Government Printing Office.

LITERATURE SELECTIONS

 Aiello, B. & Shulman, J. (1988). *Secrets Aren't Always For Keeps*. Frederick, MD: Twenty-First Century Books.

This is the story of Jennifer, a girl with a learning disability, who goes to a special resource room at school. Jennifer has a pen pal in Australia named Kay. Because of her disability, she has a friend write all her letters to Kay. When the friend tires of this, Jennifer sends Kay a tape. Finally, Kay comes to the United States with her mother for a short time. Jennifer wants to keep her learning disability a secret from Kay. However, with her father's encouragement, she decides to convey her secret. She finds out that Kay already knows (since her mother knew) and that she understands. Jennifer is delighted that she can be honest with her friend.

 • Invite a travel agent in to talk about visiting Australia.

• Kay is from Australia. Gather information about Australia. List five interesting facts about the "Land Down Under" on a bulletin board.

• Did you ever have a secret that you wanted to share with a friend? Did you share it?

• Find a pen pal—maybe in another class or school—that you can communicate with regularly. Share what you find out about your pen pal with the class.

- When Jennifer has to leave the class to go to the resource room she is embarrassed. What could you say to her to make her feel better?

- In the back of the book are questions about being disabled. What other questions do you have?

- Was Melody a good friend to Jennifer when she decided not to write her letters anymore?

- Think about what helps you to learn better. Write about this in a journal entry.

- Jennifer recorded a letter to Kay. Try the same thing—tape a message to a friend or a letter to your pen pal or someone else who would enjoy hearing from you.

- Kay uses some interesting Australian expressions. Make a list of them and their meanings.

- Kay's message says that secrets were meant for friends to share. Write a poem about a special friend.

- Try reading the stories on p. 39 and doing the activity on p. 40 to find out what having a learning disability might be like.

 Birdseye, T. (1993). *Just Call Me Stupid.* New York: Holiday House.

Patrick Lowe is a fifth-grade student who still cannot read. His classmates and even his father, who has deserted the family, called him "stupid." Patrick retreats to his own special world, where he is a brave white knight and where no one bothers him. Finally, a girl named Celina moves in next door. She loves to read and believes that Patrick can learn and is smart. She gives him the courage to prove himself at the end of the book when, challenged by the class bully, he tells his prize-winning story to the school. Patrick soon discovers that he can read.

 • Patrick's favorite story is *The Sword and the Stone.* Invite children to tell about their favorite books. Make a bulletin board display of the titles of the class's favorite books.

 • Make "I Can" books with your children. They should write about or draw things that they are able to do.

- Celina is a special friend to Patrick. Tell about someone who has been a special friend to you, someone who "believes" in you.

- Patrick has a wonderful imagination. Like Patrick did, tell a story to a peer. Record the telling. Try to write the story down.

- Mrs. Ramero is a special teacher to Patrick. Tell or write about a teacher you have had that made you feel special.

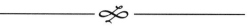

 Blue, R. (1979). *Me and Einstein.* **New York: Human Sciences Press.**

Bobby is in the fourth grade now, and is having a hard time "faking it" when reading, like he did in earlier grades. When he starts to misbehave, he is moved to a "special" class. Bobby has a hard time adjusting to this class and runs away. Finally, his parents have him tested and it is discovered that Bobby has dyslexia. The doctor recommends the Einstein School, named for Albert Einstein who also had dyslexia. Bobby goes to this school, is happy, and begins to learn how to read.

 • Provide an example of what text looks like to someone with a learning disability.

 • Invite a school psychologist in to talk about and demonstrate some of the tests that were administered to Bobby.

- Bobby ran away from home. Have you ever thought about running away? Read aloud *The Runaway Bunny* by Margaret Wise Brown and talk about how the Runaway Bunny and Bobby are alike and different.

- Bobby got in the car with the Morrisons to go to the beach. Should he have done that without talking with his parents?

- Do you think it is hard for Bobby to "fake it" when he looks at a book and pretends to read? Did you ever have to pretend to be able to do something when you couldn't? How did it feel?

- Bobby's favorite sweatshirt made him feel important. Design a t-shirt or sweatshirt. Use fabric paints to create your special shirt.

- Bobby's aunt is very special to him. Why? Write a paragraph about "My Special Friend."

- Bobby's new school was named for Albert Einstein. Several other famous people are mentioned as having dyslexia. Select one person, gather some information about him/her, and list five important facts or write a short report about that person.

Dewitt, J. (1984). *Jamie's Turn.* **Milwaukee: A Carnival Press Book, Raintree Publishers.**

Jamie Dewitt's family lives on a sixty-four-acre dairy farm near Ontario, Wisconsin. This book tells the true (and tragic) story of a farming accident and how Jamie saved his stepfather's life. Jamie went on to do many farm chores to help maintain his family's farm during his stepfather's long recovery.

Jamie's Turn is the first prize winner in Raintree's "Publish-a-Book Contest" and is nicely illustrated. There is no mention of Jamie's learning disability in the narrative—only in the notes on the last page.

 • Jamie knew what to do in an emergency. Review emergency procedures for various situations. Basic first aid and CPR could be addressed and demonstrated by the school nurse or a guest speaker.

 • Gather information about farms. Cooperative groups could research farm equipment, breeds of farm animals, crops grown in various areas around the world, use of technology in farming, environmental concerns, etc. Share information through presentations.

 • How big is sixty-four acres? Contact the city or county engineering office and ask for the boundaries that enclose approximately sixty-four acres near your school. Highlight the area on a local area map. Drive around the parcel on the way back from a field trip or send the information to parents and encourage them to point out the area.

 • Discuss safety procedures for relevant situations—bicycle riding, walking, fire prevention, etc. For example, Jamie is not wearing a helmet as he rides his motor bike.

 • Write to Raintree Publishers for information about how to submit manuscripts for the "Publish-a-Book Contest".

 • Jamie's learning disability does not interfere with his ability to think quickly and help Butch. Discuss learning disabilities and classroom implications.

• Jamie has a learning disability that makes it difficult to write (according to the information in the back of the book). He must tell his story orally. Tell a story that is important to you.

• Draw a picture of what you might have done if you were Jamie. How might you have helped Butch?

Dinneen, M. H. and the students from Deephaven School's Learning Lab. (1992). *If They Can Do It, We Can Too! Kids Writing About Famous People Who Overcame Learning Differences Similar to Theirs.* **Minneapolis: Deaconess Press.**

This book is a compilation of reports written about famous people who have learning difficulties by children who have similar learning differences. A photograph and description of each child is included. The students are all from Deephaven Elementary School in the Minnetonka school district of Minnesota.

 • Invite a successful adult who experienced learning difficulties in to share them with your students.

• Write a letter to one of the famous people included in the book. You should tell about yourself, that you've read about him or her in this book, and ask any questions that you have.

• Identify someone who is similar to you or whom you emulate. Write a letter to that person telling about yourself and asking any questions that you have.

• Interview your parents about how they learned to read and write and any difficulties that they experienced in school.

 Durn, A. B. (1993). *Trouble With School: A Family Story About Learning Disabilities.* **Bethesda, MD: Woodbine House.**

Kathryn Boesel Durn and her daughter Allison tell the story of their experience with Allison's learning disability. On facing pages, they describe the experience from their perspectives—"Allison's Mother's Story" on one page and "Allison's Story" on the other. The story focuses on Allison's second-grade year, the diagnosis, IEP development and implementation, the grade retention decision, and future plans. While Allison clearly describes her feelings, her mother offers valuable insights and suggestions to parents and teachers.

 • When Allison was in first grade, she pretended that she could read like everyone else. How do you think she felt when she was pretending? Why didn't she like going to school? Talk with children about days when they don't want to come to school.

 • Invite a school psychologist to talk with students about learning differences, testing, and/or why children receive services.

 • Allison's learning disabilities teacher explained things in different ways. Have students work in small groups to help each other understand a science or social studies concept in several different ways. Students could be encouraged to talk, write, draw, dramatize, etc.

- It was decided that Allison should repeat the second grade because it would be in her "best interests." Make a list of reasons that you think her parents and teacher gave her for that decision.

- Allison's story ends with her thinking about her third grade studies. Make a list of things that you want to learn.

 Dwyer, K. M. (1991). *What Do You Mean I Have a Learning Disability?* **New York: Walker.**

Jimmy is a ten-year-old boy who has a difficult time with many things, both in school and out of school. He just accepts the fact that other kids, including his two brothers, can do things better than he can. Jimmy thinks that he is "stupid." Finally, one of his teachers recommends that Jimmy be tested and it is discovered that he has a learning disability. After working with a tutor, Jimmy overcomes his problem. Readers will enjoy this true story of a courageous boy.

 • Jimmy's teacher asks everyone to write a paragraph about "feelings." Invite students to write about the same topic and share their paragraphs in community circle.

 • Jimmy's mom tells stories of when he was little. Ask students to bring in photos of themselves as babyies or young children and write a story about the picture. Create a class book or bulletin board.

- Jimmy has a "true best friend" in Tom. Draw a picture of you and one of your best friends doing something you both enjoy.

- Why do you think that Jimmy starts fighting in school?

- Jimmy has a secret that he shares with Ebenezer the cat. Do you have a special pet that you confide in?

- Listed in the back of the book are "Other People with Learning Disabilities." Do some research on one of the people and report your findings orally to the class.

- Write to one of the organizations in the back of the book under "Sources of Help" for more information on learning disabilities.

Gehret, J. (1990). *Learning Disabilities and the Don't-Give-Up Kid.* New York: Verbal Images Press.

Alex wants to be a famous inventor. He knows all about Thomas Edison and has already begun working on some of his own inventions. Alex is a first grader who can do many things well, but is having great difficulty reading. The letters seem to jump all over the page and flip backward and upside down. After Alex is diagnosed with a learning disability, he receives special reading instruction from Mrs. Baxter. This proves to be a wonderfully positive experience. Alex decides not to give up on reading.

- Note the introduction and the information printed at the end of the book.

- Alex wants to become a famous inventor when he grows up. Write or draw about what you want to be when you grow up.

- Alex and his dad read about Thomas Edison. Read a story about Edison or about someone you admire.

- Mrs. Baxter helped Alex read better. Write about someone who helped you learn something that was difficult for you.

- Alex realizes that other children need help with other things. What do you need help with?

 Herold, A. B. (1990). *The Hard Life of Seymour E. Newton.* Scottsdale, PA: Herald Press.

Peter, a third-grade student, has learning disabilities in writing and spelling. He is in a special class at his new school. Peter dislikes school and particularly wants to stay away from the class bully. Peter is heartened by a spider he names Seymour and by finding out that his father has learning problems similar to his own.

- Make a "web" (semantic map) about spiders with the class (where they live, what they eat, physical characteristics, etc.).

- Seymour rebuilt his web when he had to. What do you think Peter learned from this?

- Peter built a web out of an old picture frame and button thread. Try making a web by gluing yarn to construction paper.

- Peter helped his father with math because he was so good at math. What special talents do you have? What could you help a parent or other person with?

- Peter named the spider Seymour. Tell about a family pet's name. Why was he or she given that name?

- The computer helped Peter with his writing and spelling. Try typing your spelling words on the computer.

 Kraus, R. (1971). *Leo the Late Bloomer.* **New York: Simon & Schuster.**

Leo couldn't do anything right. His mother said he was just a late bloomer. His father watches to see if he will bloom. In his own time, Leo does bloom and can read, write, and draw. Young readers will enjoy all of the characters in this book, since they are animals.

- Before reading the story aloud, examine the cover with children and discuss the possible meaning of the title. Following the reading, talk about the meaning of "late bloomer." Children may discover that they were late bloomers in some areas—learning to ride a bike, learning math facts, etc.

- Is there something that you've not been able to do that your friends have? Write about that experience.

- Make a list of all the things that you can do and make it into an "I Can" book.

- Is there something that you would like to be able to do? Write about how you plan to accomplish that.

- Do you think Leo's mother and father were worried about him at the beginning of the book?

- Leo encourages us to try things that we think we can't do. What does Leo encourage you to do?

 Lasker, J. (1974). *He's My Brother.* **Morton Grove, IL: Albert Whitman.**

In this story, a young boy describes the school and home experiences of his younger brother who has a learning disability. The story presents both social and academic frustrations, along with his successes. The love and understanding that Jamie's family members show will encourage the reader to be more accepting of those with learning problems.

 • Invite a school psychologist or learning disabilities teacher in to do a simulation that would give children some sense of having a learning disability. Talk about the experience and how children learn differently.

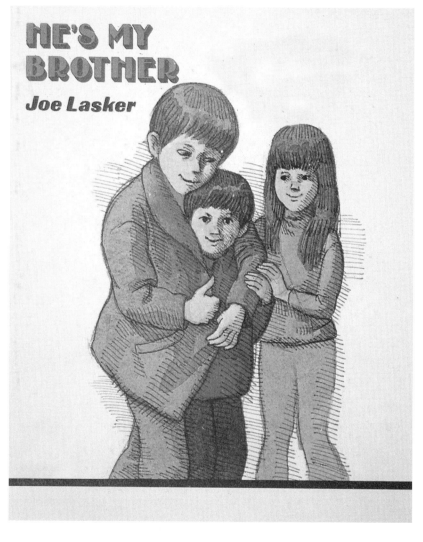

Figure 8-1 *He's My Brother* by J. Lasker (1974). Cover reprinted by permission of Albert Whitman.

- Facilitate a story writing experience. Ask children to write a story and create a book about someone in their family using *He's My Brother* as a model.

- Jamie sometimes feels left out. Write or tell about a time when you felt left out. What made you feel beter?

- Make a list of things that people in Jamie's family do to help him feel better.

- Make a list of adjectives that describe Jamie.

- Sometimes Jamie has a bad day at school. Tell or write about one of your bad days.

- If you were a friend of Jamie's, what could you do so that he would not be teased so frequently?

- Jamie imagines what it would be like to be friends with all the animals of the world. Complete this sentence: "Wouldn't it be nice if . . ." Draw a picture to accompany your image.

- Jamie plays his drums loudly when he gets frustrated. What do you like to do when you get frustrated?

- Jamie's family helps him a lot. Draw a picture of something that your family has done to help you.

 Lewis, M. (1984). *Wrongway Applebaum.* **New York: Coward-McCann.**

Stanley Applebaum, a fifth grader, really wants to play baseball. His learning disability, however, makes it difficult for him to bat and catch as well as read and write. Joining the local baseball league is so important to Applebaum that he gets his grandmother, an avid baseball fan, to sponsor and coach the team.

- There are several references throughout the book about girls being as good as boys at sports. Do a class survey. Gather information about the sports that girls and boys watch and participate in. Graph the results.

- Stanley Applebaum is called Applebaum by his friends and Stan by his dad when they play baseball. Do you have any nicknames? What do you prefer to be called? Ask your parents if they had nicknames when they were younger.

- Applebaum sometimes dreamed of being a famous baseball player. His grandmother, Sophie, dreamed of owning and coaching a baseball team. What are your dreams? Make a list of 3–5 things that you hope to accomplish.

- Sophie's hobby is baseball. What is your hobby? Draw a picture of you pursuing your hobby. Do you think "The Purls" was a good name for the team? What was Applebaum's real talent? What sports do you think he should play?

- Applebaum's team selected a team name and emblem. Design an emblem and select a name for your favorite sports team or event.

- Applebaum discovered that he was a very good runner. Draw a picture of you doing something that you do well.

- Pretend that you are one of Applebaum's teammates. Write a conversation that you might have with him as he struggled with his baseball.

- Applebaum not only has difficulty with baseball, but also with reading and spelling. Interview your teacher or a specialist in learning disabilities to find out how Applebaum could be helped.

- Sometimes Applebaum feels uncomfortable with the other kids. He is afraid they will laugh at him. Have you ever felt uncomfortable in your classroom? Why?

- One of the boys, Edward, says of Applebaum, "It would be hard to be friends with someone who was such a jerk." What would you say to Edward?

 Polacco, P. (1998). *Thank You, Mr. Falker.* New York: Philomel Books.

In this autobiographical sketch, the author recounts her own story of a little girl named Trisha who cannot learn to read, even though her grandfather has promised her that she will. The children in her class are mean to her, calling her "dummy" and "toad." In the fifth grade, a special teacher named Mr. Falker recognizes her artistic talent and helps her learn to read. Trisha is ecstatic over her new ability and the knowledge that she can now gain. The book is a lovely story and a wonderful tribute to special teachers.

- Invite a learning disabilities teacher to explain more about learning disabilities and some ways those with learning disabilities might be taught to read.

- This book is a tribute to Mr. Falker, a special teacher. Write a letter to one of your teachers telling him or her why he or she is special to you.

- Trisha has a hard time reading, but is a good artist. Tell what you are good at.

- Trisha has a special relationship with her grandparents. Tell about someone who is special in your life.

- Trisha had to move to a new school. Tell about a time when you moved or were involved in an activity where you didn't know anyone.

 Roby, C. (1994). *When Learning is Tough: Kids Talk About Their Learning Disabilities.* Morton Grove, IL: Albert Whitman.

This book includes the personal stories of eight children—five boys and three girls—who have learning disabilities. The theme that runs through each account is the feelings each child has of being "dumb," until he or she receives the appropriate help. At the end of each story, there is a "tip" provided by the child to help those with and without learning disabilities. Black and white photographs enhance the text of this book.

 - Facilitate a discussion about the things that individual students do well. They could draw a picture or bring in photographs of these activities and place these pictures on an "I Can" bulletin board.

 - Invite the school psychologist in to speak about learning disabilities. Perhaps invite an older child to come and tell his or her story of coping with learning disabilities.

- If you could give a "tip" to other children about learning, what would it be? Share your tips with the class. A Tip Sheet could be created and posted in the classroom or copies given to everyone.

- Some of the children feel that they are "dumb" because of their learning disability. However, we all feel dumb sometimes or when doing certain things. When have you felt that you needed extra help with something?

- Write to one of the organizations in the back of the book for information on learning disabilities.

Root, A. & Gladden, L. (1995). *Charlie's Challenge*. Temple, TX: U.S.A. Printmaster Press.

Charlie is a little boy who can design an award-winning castle, excels at soccer, and yet has a hard time learning to read and spell. With the help of his parents, his teacher, and a neuropsychologist, Charlie learns about his "learning difference" and how he can meet the challenge of the classroom. Special learning tests help him compensate for his learning disability.

 • Invite a neuropsychologist to class to explain about learning differences.

 • Invite a school psychologist in to demonstrate and discuss various assessment procedures and different ways of learning.

- Charlie likes to build things, especially castles. Collect materials (paper, fabric, paper towel rolls, etc.) and build different types of structures.

- Why do Charlie's classmates make fun of him in the classroom?

- Try "sky writing" your name. Why do you think this helps Charlie learn?

- Write to one of the "Sources for Help" listed in the back of the book for more information on learning disabilities.

- Charlie entered the "Best Ever Castle Building contest." Design or build a castle using Legos or something similar.

- Charlie felt better when he snuggled up to his dog. What do you do when you need to feel better? Draw and write about it.

- Dr. Fisher explains to Charlie that "We all face challenges." Write a story about a challenge you faced and how you handled it.

- Charlie finds that skywriting helps him remember his spelling words. What technique do you use to study spelling?

 Schlieper, A. (1995). *The Best Fight*. Morton Grove, IL: Albert Whitman.

Jamie, a fifth grader, has had difficulty with reading since the first grade. Fighting—his response to his classmates' teasing—results in trips to the principal's office. Mr. Wilson helps Jamie confront and deal with his reading disability and indirectly strengthens Jamie's relationship with his father as well.

 • Jamie's father explained that he also had difficulty learning to read. Working in cooperative groups, students could ask 5–7 people about how they learned to read, record their findings, and present them.

- Jamie thinks that Ms. Clayton says to everyone, "You're doing great work. Keep it up." Make a list of the comments that your teacher makes to students in your class.

- Jamie has a lot of trouble with reading, but is a very good hockey player. What do you do very well, and what is difficult for you? Make two lists. Put a star next to the items that are most important to you.

Figure 8-2   *The Best Fight* by A. Schlieper (1995). Cover reprinted by permission of Albert Whitman.

- Steven and Jamie are great friends. Write a paragraph explaining why you think they're friends.

- Mr. Wilson refers to Jamie's reading disability as a "burden." Many people have burdens. Make a list of people—famous or not—and describe their burdens. Do you have any burdens?

- Jamie and his father usually talked sitting side by side watching something. Is there a special way or place that you talk with one of your parents about important things? Write about it or draw it.

 Smith, D. B. (1975). *Kelly's Creek.* New York: Thomas Y. Crowell.

Kelly, a nine-year-old boy, has a visual perception problem that inhibits his ability to learn in school. However, a special friend teaches him about the creek and the creatures that inhabit it, and Kelly learns quickly. Given the chance to tell his class about the creek, Kelly gains their respect and moves one step closer to solving his problem.

 • Kelly has a learning disability that involves visual perception. Invite a specialist into your class to further explain learning disabilities.

- Phillip is a good friend to Kelly. Tell about a special friend that you have.

- Do you think that being restricted from the creek was a good way to get Kelly to study more?

- The creek is a special place for Kelly—a place where he can get away and do what he enjoys doing. Do you have a special place? Where is it?

- In spite of his learning problems, Kelly is good at many things. What are some things that he can do well?

- Was it a good idea for Kelly to tell the class about the fiddlers? Why?

 Swenson, J. H. & Kunz, R. B. (1986). *Learning My Way: I'm a Winner!* Minneapolis: Dillon Press.

This is the story of Don, written in the first person. Don tells of the struggles to understand his learning disability—how he came to be tested, the special programs for him at school, and ways in which he has learned to compensate. In spite of his problems, Don tries to focus on his many strengths.

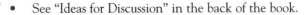

 • See "Ideas for Discussion" in the back of the book.

 • See "Funwork Activities" in the back of the book.

 • On p. 38 of the book are "Symptoms of Learning Disabilities." Invite a medical professional to further explain signs and manifestations of learning disabilities.

• Some very famous people such as Bruce Jenner, Whoopi Goldberg, and Albert Einstein have had learning disabilities. Gather information about one of these people or about another famous person who has a learning disability.

• Don's grandfather is an important person in his life. Write about an important person in your life.

• Don's grandfather said, "A person who keeps trying is always a winner." Tell about a time when you kept trying even when it was very hard for you.

CHAPTER 9

LITERATURE ABOUT CHILDREN WITH SERIOUS EMOTIONAL DISTURBANCE

Several names for this condition, such as behavioral or emotional disorder, are commonly used. The Individuals with Disabilities Education Act (IDEA) uses the term "seriously emotionally disturbed," and defines it as follows:

> (i) a condition exhibiting one or more of the following characteristics over a long period of time and to a marked degree, which adversely affects educational performance:
> (A) An inability to learn which cannot be explained by intellectual, sensory or health factors;
> (B) An inability to build or maintain satisfactory relationships with peers and teachers;
> (C) Inappropriate types of behavior or feelings under normal circumstances;
> (D) A general pervasive mood of unhappiness or depression; or
> (E) A tendency to develop physical symptoms or fears associated with personal or school problems.
> (ii) The term includes children who are schizophrenic. The term does not include children who are socially maladjusted, unless it is determined that they are seriously disturbed. (cited in Hardman, Drew, & Winston-Egan, 1996)

According to the Nineteenth Annual Report to Congress on the Implementation of the Individuals with Disabilities Education Act (IDEA), approximately 438,150 children are identified as having a serious emotional disturbance, approximately nine percent of the total number of children with disabilities.

Although there are several classification systems for serious emotional disturbances, a generally accepted one describes two broad categories of problems: externalizing and internalizing behaviors (Achenbach & Edelbrock, 1981). Externalizing behavior problems, the more common, include persistent aggression, acting out, and noncompliant behaviors. These actions may be overt (for example, destructiveness) or covert (for example, lying and stealing). Internalizing behavior problems include social withdrawal, depression, and anxiety.

Some students who are seriously emotionally disturbed present a real challenge in an inclusive setting because of intense interventions that may be needed. For this reason, many are educated in more restrictive environments such as self-contained classrooms or even residential facilities. However, some general education teachers are very successful teaching students with serious emotional disturbance in their classes. This involves working not only on improving academic skills, but on social skills as well. The teacher must be well versed in structured classroom management, as these students are often in need of a systematic, consistent, and predictable system.

The literature selections are somewhat different from those in other chapters, in that the main character is not identified as having a serious emotional disturbance, but might have extreme emotions (such as anger) or be in a situation that could potentially cause or be related to an emotional or behavioral problem. For example, several selections deal with children in an abusive situation, which puts them at risk for developing disruptive behavior disorders. Discussion should revolve around ways for individuals in these situations to get help.

REFERENCES

Achenbach, T. M., & Edelbrock, C. S. (1981). Behavior problems and competencies reported by parents of normal and disturbed children aged four through sixteen. *Monographs of the Society for Research in Child Development, 46*(1), serial no. 188.

Hardman, M. L., Drew, C. J., & Winston-Egan, M. (1996). *Human exceptionality: Society, School, and Family.* Boston: Allyn & Bacon.

LITERATURE SELECTIONS

 Foster, C.H. (1994). *Polly's Magic Games: A Child's View of Obsessive-Compulsive Disorder.* Ellsworth, ME: Dilligaf.

Although Polly, age ten, is very much like her friend Annie, she discovers that she does some different things. She counts every step on her way up the stairs, turns the bathroom light switch on and off exactly five times, and washes her hands so much that they turn red. Following a disagreement with Annie and a talk with her mother, Polly is diagnosed with obsessive-compulsive disorder. They hope that vitamins, medicine, and patience will provide successful treatment. "A Note to Parents and Friends" is included at the end of the book offering helpful suggestions.

- Talk with students about differences and how they should talk with someone if they have a question about themselves or someone else.

- Polly and Annie are great friends and are quite similar. Select one or two of your friends. Make a Venn diagram illustrating your likenesses and differences.

Figure 9-1 *Polly's Magic Games* by C. H. Foster (1994). Cover reprinted by permission of the author.

- Polly has a long talk with her mom about her problem. Write a letter to one of your parents, your teacher, or another adult about something special about yourself.

- One of the girls' favorite summer treats is orange popsicles. What is your favorite summer treat? Survey your classmates. Make a bar graph to display the results.

 Lowery, L. (1994). *Laurie Tells.* **Minneapolis: Carolrhoda Books.**

Laurie is an eleven-year-old girl who is distraught over the sexual abuse she is suffering at the hands of her father. She tried to tell her mother, but her mother told her not to "get carried away by your imagination." Laurie finally tells her Aunt Jan, who promises to help her so that the abuse will never happen again. The text and lovely illustrations depict this topic sensitively.

 • Initiate a discussion about "good touching" and "bad touching." What can you do if someone touches you in a bad way? (Look at the "Author's Note" in the back of the book for additional discussion ideas.)

- Aunt Jan was very special to Laurie. Tell about someone special whom you can trust.

- Laurie has mixed emotions about her father. Imagine you are Laurie and write a letter to your dad.

- In small groups, make a list of other people who could help someone in such a situation.

 Simon, N. (1974). *I Was So Mad.* **Morton Grove, IL: Albert Whitman.**

The text and illustrations in this book depict situations that result in such reactions as frustration, anxiety, humiliation, and loss of control for the main character, a little girl. For example, she "gets mad" when someone knocks down her blocks, teases her, or tells her to try some food she doesn't like.

 • Initiate a discussion about feelings. What kinds of things make you mad? Do you think it was appropriate for the girl in this story to get mad over the things described?

- In small groups, discuss what you can do when you feel very angry. Share your discussion with the whole class.

- What can you do for a classmate who gets extremely angry?

- Draw a picture of yourself resolving anger in an appropriate way.

 Stanek, M. (1983). *Don't Hurt Me, Mama.* **Morton Grove, IL: Albert Whitman.**

The little girl in this story tells how her father had left her and her mother, so they had to move to an apartment in the city. Mama can't find a job, and often "gets mean," hitting the little girl. A kind and sensitive school nurse sees that this young victim of child abuse and her abusing mother get help.

- Invite a social worker to class to explain why people sometimes abuse others and what can be done to help them.

- Going to church made the little girl happy. Draw a picture of yourself in a place that makes you happy. Share your picture with the class.

- The school nurse is one person who is a helper to us. Who are some other people who can help us in difficult situations?

- Continue this story. Write what you think will happen to Mama and the little girl after they get the help they need.

 Trotter, M. (1997). *A Safe Place.* **Morton Grove, IL: Albert Whitman.**

A young girl named Emily tells the story of waking up in a strange place one morning. Then she recounts her story of coming to this safe place when Mama and Daddy had fought one night. She sees many children and mothers at the house, each with special jobs to do there. She misses her dad, but together, she and her mother start a new life when they leave the security of the shelter.

- Invite someone from a women's shelter to explain the purposes for such a facility.

- Write a letter to Emily in which you ask her questions you have about the safe place.

- Tell about a time when you felt scared. What made you scared? What made you feel safe again?

- Emily has a special bear she takes to the safe place. Do you have a special toy? Tell about it.

Vigna, J. (1988). *I Wish Daddy Didn't Drink So Much*. Morton Grove, IL: Albert Whitman.

Lisa is a little girl who has a disappointing Christmas because her father fails to keep his promise to take her sledding with the new sled he built her. Lisa's father is an alcoholic, and with the help of a good friend and her mother, Lisa learns how to deal with his alcoholism.

- Have children write to one of the organizations listed in the back of the book for additional information on children of alcoholics.

- The holiday was disappointing for Lisa. She wishes she could have a "real Christmas like other people." Tell about one of your favorite holidays.

- Make up a play to tell the story in the book.

- Use puppets to tell the story in the book.

CHAPTER 10

LITERATURE ABOUT CHILDREN WITH AUTISM

In 1975, PL 94-142 classified autism as a subcategory of the larger category of serious emotional disturbance. In response to objection from the Autism Society of America, in 1981 Congress placed autism into the category of "other health impairments." Finally in 1990, Congress identified autism as a separate category in the Individuals with Disabilities Education Act (IDEA) and defined it the following way:

> Autism means a developmental disability significantly affecting verbal and nonverbal communication and social interaction, generally evident before age 3, that adversely affects educational performance. Other characteristics often associated with autism are engagement in repetitive activities and stereotypical movements, resistance to environmental change or changes in daily routines, and unusual responses to sensory experiences. The term does not apply if a child's educational performance is adversely affected primarily because the child has a serious emotional disturbance. (Turnbull, Turnbull, Shank, & Leal, 1995, p. 330)

According to the Nineteenth Annual Report to Congress on the Individuals with Disabilities Education Act (1997), approximately 28,827 children between the ages of six and twenty-one are identified as having autism, one percent of the total number of children with disabilities.

Implications for the curriculum for students with autism vary since many of those with autism also have mental retardation, whereas others have average or above average intellectual functioning (a small percentage of those with autism are savants, who have extreme abilities usually in one area). In general, whether fully included or not, a student with autism should be educated in a calm, structured setting, where much attention is paid to both language and social development. It is also imperative for the teacher to understand and be able to apply positive behavioral support, a technique for creating a positive, responsive environment (Horner, Dunlap, Koegel, Carr, Sailor, Anderson, Albin, & O'Neill, 1990). Positive behavioral support recognizes that problem behaviors often stem from someone else's failure to provide individualized support. Rather than mechanistically applying rewards and punishments, positive behavioral support seeks to create an environment tailored to the personal preferences, strengths, and needs of the individuals with problem behaviors.

One controversial procedure to help those with autism is facilitated communication, brought to the United States from Australia by Douglas Biklen. With facilitated communication, one person (a facilitator), supports the arm of another as he or she uses a keyboard to communicate (Biklen, 1992). The controversy lies in a question of the origin of the communicated message—the person with autism or the facilitator. While a definitive answer is not yet available, it is important to look at the implications about those for whom facilitated communication does work—that they can communicate in some capacity.

There are very few current books available featuring children with autism. The literature selections that follow inform the reader about the characteristics and the learning needs of those with autism.

REFERENCES

Biklen, D. (1992). Typing to talk: Facilitated communication. *American Journal of Speech-Language Pathology. 1*(2), 15–17.

Horner, R. H., Dunlap, G., Koegel, R. L., Carr, E.G., Sailor, W., Anderson, J., Albin, R. W., & O'Neill, R. E. (1990). Toward a technology of "nonaversive" behavioral support. *Journal of the Association for Persons with Severe Handicaps. 15*(3), 125–132.

Turnbull, A. P., Turnbull, H. R., Shank, M., & Leal, D. (1995). *Exceptional lives: Special education in today's schools.* Englewood Cliffs, NJ: Merrill, an imprint of Prentice Hall.

U.S. Department of Education. (1997). Nineteenth annual report to Congress on the implementation of the Individuals with Disabilities Education Act. Washington, DC: U.S. Government Printing Office.

LITERATURE SELECTIONS

 Amenta, C. A., (1992). *Russell Is Extra Special: A Book about Autism for Children.* New York: Magination Press.

Photographs and clearly written text describe the author's son who has autism. The book discusses various aspects of autistic behavior. The author provides an informative "Introduction for Parents."

 • Invite a physician or other health professional to further explain autism.

 • Russell uses some sign language for what he wants. Teach the children a few signs for common objects or needs. Make a children's sign language book available for those who may want to learn more on their own.

- Russell likes to be alone most of the time. When do you like to be alone? Draw a picture or write about what you enjoy doing alone.

- Sometimes Russell causes problems or gets into trouble. Write a story about a time that you got into trouble.

- A family photo appears on the last page of the book. Draw a picture of your family or bring in a photograph. Identify each person and write something.

- Russell often has a difficult time at night. It's hard to know if he is afraid or just tired. Have you ever had a hard time sleeping? Why?

- Make a list of all the things that Russell can do well.

- What are some ways that Russell's family could help him around the house?

 Gold, P. (1975). *Please Don't Say Hello.* New York: Human Sciences Press.

The Masons have just moved into their new house with their son Eddie, who has autism. The neighborhood boys are struggling to understand why Eddie has so many fears, spins his coins constantly, and will not look at them. Mrs. Mason explains the puzzling world of autism to them. Through this exploration and the boys' visit to Eddie's special school, the reader comes to understand the characteristics of his disability.

- Write to the National Society for Autistic Children (address is on the back of the front cover) for more information on autism. Share the information with students or invite a specialist to discuss this disability with the class.

- How did the boys react to Eddie? Why?

- What kinds of things might they work on at Eddie's school?

- Everyone has special abilities in spite of problems. What special abilities does Eddie have?

- The book explains that the word autism comes from the Greek word "autos," meaning "self." How does this apply to the disability of autism?

Katz, I. (1993). *Joey and Sam.* Northridge, CA: Real Life Storybooks.

This book focuses on a family with two young sons—six-year-old Joey and five-year-old Sam. Joey has conflicting emotions about Sam, who has autism. He asks, "Why can't he be like other brothers?" Joey and Sam go to the same school, where Sam is in a class with five other children with autism. During a school performance, Sam reads a poem and dances before the entire school, and Joey is very proud of him. He tells him, "I love you the way you are!"

- Note the information section on the last page of the book. Share some of this information with the class.

- Miss Terry and Mr. Reed are special teachers who help Sam learn things. Interview a special teacher at your school to see how he or she helps children with special needs.

- Do you think that Sam knew more than he was able to show? Give some examples that make you think this.

- Continue this story. Will Joey be ashamed of or embarrassed by Sam from now on?

 Lears, L. (1998). *Ian's Walk—A Story About Autism.* Morton Grove, IL: Albert Whitman.

Ian is described by his older sister Julie as someone whose "brain doesn't work like other people's." He sees, hears, smells, feels, and tastes things differently. Ian goes for a walk to the park with his two sisters and disappears as they're waiting for pizza. When Julie thinks the way Ian does, she finds him lying under a huge bell ringing the gong. They are so relieved to find Ian that they walk home his way—lining up stones at the pond, smelling the bricks of the post office, and watching the fan at the diner. Julie thinks she sees Ian smile when they finally get home.

- Encourage a discussion of how Ian does things differently. Ask children if they do something that they or others think is unusual.

- Ian watches the ceiling fan in the diner, smells the bricks of the post office wall, feels the stones on the ground press against his cheek as he lies on the ground, and chooses to eat dry cereal rather than fast food. Try some of the things that Ian finds interesting.

- Ian prefers dry cereal to fast food. Survey students in your class or school about their favorite snacks. Display the results in a graph.

- Julie and Tara think that Ian is lost. Have you ever disappeared from your parents or someone who was taking care of you? Draw or write about what happened.

- If you could do something special with your brother, sister, or friend, what would it be? Make a card inviting him or her to do that activity.

Figure 10-1 *Ian's Walk* by L. Lears (1998). Cover reprinted by permission of Albert Whitman & Company.

 Martin, A. (1990). *Kristy and the Secret of Susan.* **New York: Scholastic.**

Kristy, the president of the Baby Sitters Club, has a new job babysitting Susan, an eight-year-old girl with autism. When she first meets Susan, she describes her as "reluctant-looking," a girl who made "strange gestures and movements." As Kristy finds out more about Susan, she discovers that she is a savant, and has a remarkable talent for playing the piano and also has a "calendar in her head." Kristy, seeing some students with disabilities who participate in regular activities at her own school, wonders why Susan is sent away to a special school. Finally, Kristy realizes the truly special help that Susan needs at her school and even thinks that when she grows up, she will be a teacher to help children like Susan.

 • Invite the students to research more about autism and savants. What are some of the characteristics of autism? What special talents might savants have?

 • Obtain the movie "Rainman" and watch clips from it. Have the class compare the behavior of those with autism as seen in the movie and in the book.

- Kristy thinks that she can change Susan so that Susan can go to her school. Why do you think she finally realizes that she can't change Susan?

- Kristy thinks she might be a teacher when she grows up. Write about what you'd like to be.

- Susan has special talents playing the piano and knowing all about calendars. What special talents do you have?

- Continue this story. How will Susan relate to her new baby sister? Will Susan be a concert pianist?

 Thompson, M. (1996). *Andy and His Yellow Frisbee.* **Bethesda, MD: Woodbine House.**

Andy is a young boy with autism who spends his recess time spinning a yellow frisbee. Sarah, a new girl at school, is curious about why Andy spins the frisbee and gently approaches him. Rosie, Andy's sister, protectively looks on and worries about how Andy will react. He doesn't respond negatively, and Rosie is hopeful about his next encounter with Sarah. Sarah and Rosie become friends in the end.

 • Emphasize the acceptance and understanding that Sarah shows toward Andy even though she doesn't understand his behavior. Discuss the application of this acceptance with students.

• Invite a speech pathologist to class to demonstrate various augmentative communication devices for people with autism and other disabilities.

- Write to the Autism Society of America for further information on autism.

- Bring frisbees to school to play with at recess.

- Sarah has a special teddy bear that she takes with her for security. Write about a toy or object that is special to you.

 Watson, E. (1996). *Talking to Angels.* **San Diego: Harcourt, Brace, & Co.**

Christa, who has autism, sees the world in a different way than most people do. Her sister tells the story of how Christa repeats what others say and does other things that many people don't understand. A tribute to her sister with autism, the author says that Christa "talks to angels."

Figure 10-2 *Andy and His Yellow Frisbee* by M. Thompson (1996). Cover reprinted by permission of Woodbine House.

 • Show the picture of the author and her sister on the book jacket. Explain that the book is a true story about two special sisters. Encourage the children to write their story about a sister, brother, or friend.

• The illustrations in this book are almost cartoon-like. Create a cartoon, using bubbles where characters "talk" to each other or "think."

• Research autism in the encyclopedia or on the internet to find out more about it. Share your findings with classmates.

CHAPTER 11

LITERATURE ABOUT CHILDREN WITH SPEECH AND LANGUAGE IMPAIRMENT

The Individuals with Disabilities Education Act (IDEA) defines the term speech and language impairment this way:

> Speech or language impairment means a communication disorder such as stuttering, impaired articulation, a language impairment that adversely affects a child's educational performance. (cited in Turnbull, Turnbull, Shank, & Leal,1995, p. 510)

These disorders are not the result of a hearing loss and are not related to cultural differences. According to the Nineteenth Annual Report to Congress on the Implementation of the Individuals with Disabilities Education Act (1997), approximately 1,025,941 children are identified as having a speech or language impairment, twenty percent of the total number of children with disabilities.

SPEECH IMPAIRMENTS

Disorders of articulation, voice, and fluency constitute speech impairments. Articulation disorders, the largest group, occur when the student is unable to produce various sounds of the language (Hulit & Howard, 1993). Examination of typical age-appropriate development is a key to determining if there is an articulation disorder.

Voice disorders affect the quality of the voice itself. Because of structural problems, the voice may be breathy, hypernasal, or hyponasal. Other disorders of the voice include a pitch that is too high or too low and/or problems of intensity (loudness).

Disorders of fluency or stuttering are the third type of speech disorder. All children and adults are dysfluent occasionally. Normal dysfluency becomes stuttering when the disruptions are accompanied by awareness, anxiety (struggle or tension), or compensatory behaviors (Cantwell & Baker, 1987).

LANGUAGE IMPAIRMENTS

Language impairments can occur as the only disability or in combination with other disabilities.

Children with language impairments may have difficulty with one or more of the five dimensions of language:

1. phonology—grouping sounds to make meaningful words
2. morphology—using rules to contrive meaningful units into words
3. syntax—using rules to contrive words into sentences
4. semantics—understanding word meaning and using words to create meaningful sentences
5. pragmatics—using language appropriately in social contexts

A speech and/or language impairment can affect a person in many ways. According to Bashir in 1989 (cited in Turnbull et al.,1995), students with language impairment are more likely to experience academic problems. Furthermore, those who experienced language development problems as preschoolers are more likely to have problems with reading and writing and with peer and social interaction. The lack of an effective communication system can affect interaction both inside and outside the classroom.

Since the vast majority of students with speech or language impairments are in general education programs, it is important for teachers to help such a student in order to be successfully included. He or she must collaborate with the speech-language pathologist on a plan for remediation or compensation. Both must work with the family so that all are consistent in reinforcing strategies to help with the speech or language problem.

REFERENCES

Cantwell, D. P. & Baker, L. (1987). *Developmental speech and language disorders*. New York: Guilford.

Hulit, L. M. & Howard, M. R. (1993). *Born to talk*. New York: Macmillan.

Turnbull, A. P., Turnbull, H. R., Shank, M., & Leal, D. (1995). *Exceptional lives: Special education in today's schools.* Englewood Cliffs, NJ: Merrill, an imprint of Prentice Hall.

U.S. Department of Education. (1997). Nineteenth annual report to Congress on the implementation of the Individuals with Disabilities Education Act. Washington, DC: U.S. Government Printing Office.

LITERATURE SELECTIONS

 Helfman, E. (1992). *On Being Sarah.* **Morton Grove, IL: Albert Whitman.**

Twelve-year-old Sarah is in a wheelchair and uses a communication board to speak because she has spastic cerebral palsy. The story tells of her frustration with her inability to speak the words that are "in her head." It also explains her relationships with significant people in her life—her sister, mother, father, aunt, neighbor, and Johnnie (her good friend)—some of whom are willing to communicate with her and some who are not. Sarah is afraid that she might be put into an institution, since her father worries about the stress that taking care of Sarah has on her mother. In the end, Sarah goes to a new "regular" school, her relationships with those around her improve, and she realizes that sometimes words aren't needed to express feelings.

 • Invite a speech therapist to demonstrate different augmentative communication systems.

 • Discuss nonverbal communication. In pairs, have students demonstrate a message without using words.

• Sarah's relationship with her dad is not always the best. Why do you think her father has trouble accepting her?

• Johnnie is a special friend to Sarah. Write about a special friend that you have.

• Look around your school building. Is it accessible for people like Sarah who are in wheelchairs?

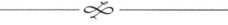

 Jupor, F. (1967). *Atu, the Silent One.* **New York: Holiday House.**

This is the story of Atu, an African boy of long ago. Atu had never learned to talk the way the other people of his tribe talked. Instead, Atu drew pictures on the sand or on rock and used sign language. Atu told his story of the great

Figure 11-1 *On Being Sarah* by E. Helfman (1993). Cover reprinted by permission of Albert Whitman.

elephant hunt in pictures on a rock. Pictures like these, drawn by the Bushmen, can still be seen today.

 • Atu drew pictures in the sand. Try some sand art.

 • The tribesmen liked to tell stories about their lives. With a partner, have students take turns telling a story to each other.

- Like Atu, draw a picture to tell a story about something.

- Atu never learned to talk, but he had other special talents. Write about one thing you do well and one thing you have problems with.

 Levy, M. N. (1991). *The Summer Kid.* **Toronto, Canada: Second Story Press.**

Ten-year-old Karen is staying at the summer cottage with only her grandmother this year, since her family can't come. She meets Tommy, a boy who acts "weird," talks slowly, and doesn't understand everything said to him. In spite of his difficulties, Tommy is good at building things, and he and Karen win a sandcastle-building contest. Karen comes to understand that Tommy has a language delay, realizes that he is as old as she is, and becomes his friend and advocate.

 • Explain further about a language delay and what that might imply for children in a class.

- Tommy has a hard time understanding certain expressions like "the sky opens up," meaning rain. Encourage students to think of some other expressions and discuss them with the class.

- Tommy is good at building sandcastles, but has a hard time with speech. What things are you good at? Make an "I Can" book.

- Karen felt that she "used" Tommy to win the sandcastle contest. What does that mean?

 Moran, G. (1994). *Imagine Me on a Sit-Ski!* **Morton Grove, IL: Albert Whitman.**

Written in the first person, Billy describes his experience learning how to sitski. Because he has cerebral palsy, he is in a wheelchair. He explains that while he understands what is said to him, he is unable to respond verbally. Instead he uses his word board. Billy has a great time skiing with a group of friends with disabilities who use a variety of equipment.

 • Visit a ski resort that offers lessons for people with disabilities or invite a ski instructor in to talk about how people with various disabilities can learn to ski.

 • Invite a speech and language pathologist to demonstrate various augmentative communication devices.

- Billy was unable to speak. Don't talk for an hour. Communicate in other ways. At the end of the hour, write a brief reflection about how you communicated and how you felt during that time.

- Billy learned that he could "wipe out and not get hurt." Write about a time that you "wiped out."

- Billy had a great time skiing and thinks he will do it again. He is also considering scuba diving. Make a list of activities or sports that you currently do and others that you would like to try someday.

- Draw a picture of yourself doing a favorite activity or sport.

 Yates, S. (1994). *Nobody Knows*. Winnepeg, Manitoba, Canada: Gemma B. Publishing.

A touching story, Ann is a six-year-old girl with cerebral palsy that has affected her speech. She and her friend Jay adventure out into the yard where they see a turtle and an alligator. Although Ann cannot talk directly about her journey, the story is written in the first person and the reader knows what Ann is thinking.

 • Invite a physician to explain more about the implications of cerebral palsy.

• Imagine how frustrating it must be for Ann not to have people understand her. Write how you would feel in that situation.

• The man in the story says that "the cat has her tongue." Think about another expression you have heard. Illustrate your expression.

• Ann likes to ride horses. Write about or draw a picture of yourself doing an activity you enjoy.

CHAPTER 12

LITERATURE ABOUT CHILDREN WITH MULTIPLE DISABILITIES

The Individuals with Disabilities Education Act (IDEA) defines children with multiple disabilities as those with "concomitant impairments (such as mental retardation–blindness, mental retardation–orthopedic impairment), the combination of which causes such severe educational problems that they cannot be accommodated in special education solely for the purpose of one of the impairments. The term does not include deaf–blindness" (cited in Salend, 1998, p. 93).

Because of the range of needs of students with multiple disabilities, there is not a common set of characteristics that are particular to this group of individuals. Teachers need to be aware of this fact, but also of the fact that most children who are served in these programs have severe mental retardation. Thus, much of what was described in Chapter 6 on mental retardation also applies here (Turnbull, Turnbull, Shank, & Leal, 1995). Academically, these students may have extra difficulty learning new skills and generalizing to new situations. A functional curriculum would probably be a part of programming, whereby students might learn how to find items in a grocery store, for example. Adaptive behaviors are another area of significance for most of these students. They must usually be taught self-care skills such as feeding, dressing, and toileting directly, so that they can participate as fully as possible when being assisted. Social skills, often the determinant of success in independent living and adjustment, are also a critical part of instruction. Because these students may experience problems in health, sensory, communication, or motor development, additional services in these areas may be required.

Though some students with multiple disabilities are educated in more restrictive environments, many remain in the general education classroom and are given the additional supports they need within this classroom. Community inclusion is equally important to people, both young and old, with multiple disabilities. In addition, family collaboration is critical to their success.

The first literature selection portrays a little girl who is identified as having several disability areas. This is different from books featured in other chapters, which portray children with two disabilities, where one area is the primary disability area. Also included are several books featuring many children with different disabilities.

REFERENCES

Salend, S. J. (1998). *Effective mainstreaming: Creating inclusive classrooms.* Upper Saddle River, NJ: Merrill, an imprint of Prentice Hall.

Turnbull, A. P., Turnbull, H. R., Shank, M., & Leal, D. (1995). *Exceptional lives: Special education in today's schools.* Englewood Cliffs, NJ: Merrill, an imprint of Prentice Hall.

LITERATURE SELECTIONS

 Rosenberg, M. B. (1983). *My Friend Leslie: The Story of a Handicapped Child.* New York: Lothrop, Lee, and Shepard Books.

Leslie was born with a visual impairment, hearing loss, and "stiff muscles." The story is told from the viewpoint of her friend, who is in the same kindergarten class with her. It tells of the things that Leslie likes to do and things that they like to do together. The story is a warm tale of the friendship between two girls.

 • Leslie's class makes stew. Try making stew or soup with your class.

 • Make an "I Can" bulletin board using photographs of students doing something they enjoy.

• Leslie is good at many things, especially reading. What are you good at? Draw a picture of yourself doing this activity.

• The girl telling the story and Leslie are good friends. Tell about a special friend that you have.

The following books include children with a variety of disabilities. They could be used to introduce various disabilities.

 Brown, T. (1984). *Someone Special, Just Like You.* New York: Holt, Rinehart & Winston.

A beautiful photo essay, this book tells the story of many children with disabilities who have the same wants, needs, likes, and dislikes as other children.

The differences that might appear to separate them are not important. Most of the children shown are preschool children.

- Before reading the story, talk with children about some special things that they like to do.

- Bring a photograph of yourself doing a special activity. Write a paragraph about the picture.

- Write a story about the last picture in the book. What do you think is happening?

 Derby, J. (1993). *Are You My Friend?* Scottsdale, PA: Herald Press.

A little boy notices that people, although different in some ways, are also similar to him in other ways. In his search for a friend, he asks many people—including those who are deaf, those who are blind, and those who are physically larger or smaller than he is— "Are you my friend?"

- Encourage a discussion of the boy's openness to look beyond differences to the many similarities that people have.

- Write how you and a friend are both alike and different. Try making a Venn diagram to help you with your ideas.

- Write an acrostic poem about friendship. (See format in Appendix A.)

- What are some good ways to make friends? How can you be a good friend?

 Dwight, L. (1992). *We Can Do It!* Fairless Hills, PA: Checkerboard Press.

Children with many types of disabilities, including cerebral palsy, spina bifida, blindness, and Down syndrome are portrayed in this book. The beautiful photographs depict them in all types of activities—at school, at home, and with the physical therapist. Most of the children are preschool age.

- Design a collage bulletin board showing many of the things children enjoy doing.

- Look at the cover of the book. What do you think the title means?

- Do you think that most of the children in the book are happy? Why?

- Write about something new that you have learned that you are proud of.

 Exley, H. (Ed.) (1984). *What It's Like to Be Me*. New York: Friendship Press.

This book includes contributions from children with a variety of disabilities from all over the world. Art, poetry, brief comments, as well as stories included in many short sections with titles such as "Joys I'll Never Know," "Feeling Like a Stranger," and "I'm Happy To Be Me," provide honest insights into these children's lives.

 • Select entries to read to students that help them understand a classmate or that are related to a unit of study. For example, during a study of a particular country or part of the world, read entries from children who live there.

- Write a story or poem with the same title as the book, *What It's Like to Be Me*.

- A list of schools that the children attend is included at the end of the book. Select a school, write for information about the school, and tell them about your having read the book.

 McConnell, N. P. (1993). *Different and Alike*. Colorado Springs, CO: Current.

This informative book explains that people are different in many ways and that some differences are called disabilities. The book then discusses six categories of disabilities, including learning disability and blindness in separate sections. It also includes ways to help a person with a disability.

 • This book features many vocabulary words associated with disabilities. Reinforce knowledge of these terms by writing them on the board, discussing them, etc.

 • Try some of the activities suggested in the book, such as the "touch and feel" box.

- Using the finger spelling on pp. 12–13, try spelling something for a partner to figure out.

- Try some of the signs on p. 15. Show them to a parent, sibling, or friend.

- Feel the braille on p. 19 of the book. How do you think it would be to have to read this way?

- The book has some ideas for helping a person with a disability. Make a list of three other ways you could help someone. Share these with your class.

 Meyer, D. (Ed.). (1997). *Views from Our Shoes: Growing Up with a Brother or Sister with Special Needs.* Bethesda, MD: Woodbine House.

> Forty-five sisters and brothers of children with special needs share their thoughts in this book. The writers' ages range from four to eighteen and they live in eighteen different states. They tell about a range of events and feelings—the positive and the difficult. Their siblings' disabilities include autism, cerebral palsy, health problems, Attention Deficit Disorder, hydrocephalus, mental retardation, visual and hearing impairments, and Down, Angelman, Mohr, Tourette, and Rett syndromes.
>
> The editor, Donald Meyer, is the Director of the Sibling Support Project at Children's Hospital and Medical Center in Seattle, Washington. He invites siblings of children with special needs to send him their stories and includes a list of possible questions for consideration. A glossary and list of related organizations is also provided.

- Discuss (in a hypothetical way) some of the questions the editor provides at the end of the book.

- Select one of the entries and write a letter to its author.

- Write a story or poem about your brother, sister, or a special friend.

- The writers of this book tell about the good things and the difficult things about having a sibling with special needs. Select a brother, sister, or friend. Make a list of the things you especially like about that person. Give the list to him or her.

Figure 12-1 *Views From Our Shoes* by D. Meyer (ed.) (1997). Cover reprinted by permission of Woodbine House.

 Nelson, J. (1993). *Friends All Around.* Bothell, WA: The Wright Group.

This multicultural selection briefly tells about the experiences that friends share at an amusement park. Sara is deaf, Andrew has a physical disability and uses a wheelchair, Laura is blind, and Taylor has Down syndrome. They all have a wonderful time riding the merry-go-round.

 • With students, make a list of the children's names, their disability, and how they enjoy the merry-go-round.

- What is your favorite amusement park ride? What do you especially like about it? Draw a picture of the ride and write a sentence or short paragraph about it.

- Make a poster advertising your favorite amusement park ride.

- These classmates all enjoy a trip to an amusement park. Write or draw about one of your favorite class field trips.

 Smith, S.L. (1994). *Different Is Not Bad, Different Is the World: A Book About Disabilities.* Longmont, CO: Sopris West.

This book celebrates differences as it examines the idea that people look different, have different bodies, are good at different things, etc. It also discusses the fact that some people have difficulty learning and doing other things, due to a variety of disabilities. Examples of famous people with disabilities are provided.

 • Note the "Introduction" section at the beginning of the book. Several activities to do with young children are provided.

 • In small groups, have students report on the clothes, holidays, etc. of different countries.

- Draw a picture of your house. Compare and contrast it with pictures of houses on p. 2. Do you ever feel like your house is in the "wrong place" as the book suggests?

- Make signs similar to those on p. 18 that tell what different *is* rather than what it is not.

- Report on the lives of some of the people on pp. 24–25. What things are they famous for?

CHAPTER  13

FURTHER SUGGESTIONS

Deborah Wooten describes a special moment in teaching as the right book connecting with a student to meet a specific need. She goes on to tell about her experience with a sixth-grade girl whose writing displayed wonderful imagery. Wooten discovered that the girl's father was blind and that she spent a lot of time describing things to him. The book *Knots on a Counting Rope* by Bill Martin, Jr. was the perfect book for her (Wooten, D. A., 1992). Children's literature can provide students with a story similar to theirs or can provide an opportunity for them to vicariously experience something that is not an immediate part of their lives.

Although the use of children's literature featuring children with disabilities is a wonderful way to facilitate acceptance and understanding, the classroom teacher can also do other things with this objective. Creating an environment rich in literature, and incorporating some of the following components promote a successful inclusive environment.

SIMULATIONS

The use of disability-awareness activities is an effective way for students without disabilities to understand what it feels like to have a disability. One author of this text regularly uses "inclusion activities" in her college class on exceptionalities to encourage just such an understanding. There are simulations that can be used in general, and those that are specific to certain disabilities. A few were included in the literature activities, and some additional examples follow:

- The teacher can have students line up in the front of the room from left to right according to their birthdates. To accomplish this, however, they may not use their voices (to promote an understanding of deafness).

- The teacher can have students make "glasses" that prevent them from seeing clearly. Make the glasses out of index cards cut into the shape of glasses and use wax paper for the lenses. Students can wear these for a short amount of time to see what it is like to have a visual impairment.

- In pairs, students sit back-to-back. One partner draws a design on a piece of paper in front of him or her, and then tries to describe it to the other (who cannot see it), who must duplicate it on his or her paper. Students then switch roles. This activity promotes an understanding of visual impairment or communication disorder.

- Tunnel vision may be simulated by holding two paper cups with small central holes cut into them.

It might be beneficial to have students follow these activities with a writing exercise in which they describe their feelings and reactions to the simulations.

FRIENDSHIP FACILITATING ACTIVITIES

Educators and families need to use a variety of strategies to encourage the development of friendships among those with and without disabilities. Instruction about friendships can be made an integral part of the curriculum (Stainback, Stainback, & Wilkinson, 1992). This would include the importance of friendships, and ideas such as the qualities of friends and qualities of being a good friend, etc. A social skills curriculum in the primary grades can do much to instruct the students on how to make friends, how to actively listen, how to engage in conversations, and other vital skills.

The social organization in the classroom is another avenue for encouraging friendships among students. Teachers who use flexible groupings, collaborative learning, partners, or buddy systems enable students to get to know each other on a more personal basis.

Finally, the use of conflict resolution strategies in the classroom can help solve conflicts among students by giving them more ownership of their own classroom and the interactions that occur there. Sometimes peers can do much to shape the behavior of another, thus encouraging acceptance of this individual.

USE OF CURRENT ADAPTIVE DEVICES

Technological adaptations can offer a student with disabilities more individualized ways of receiving, expressing, and manipulating information. There are many possibilities for enhancing students' learning in the classroom through both hardware and software. In terms of hardware and peripherals, there are specialized keyboards for one-handed use and split ergonomic keyboards for motor issues. Other devices can angle and change the direction of the keyboard (for example, one-handed, circular keyboards). Additional adaptive devices include switches controlled by various body parts, such as eye blinks, arm, foot, head, and mouth (Surabian, 1998).

Some software allows for full sensory integration, integral to the learning of many students with disabilities. Some word processing features include variable font size and highlighting, magnification, spell checking, phonetic suggestions for spelling, word prediction, word banks, sample sentence generation, and grammar correction. There are homework helpers and textbook readers, which are scanned duplicates of lessons/textbooks/reading books for computer use with auditory and visual feedback. Other software offers thought organization for writing (for example, story mapping or webbing). There is software for language development and language disorders, for cognitive development and cognitive remediation, and for reading in special education settings (Surabian, 1998).

These represent only a fraction of the wealth of material that is available. Teachers and parents can do much to enhance the educational experience of students with disabilities through the use of assistive technologies. (See also Appendix E for web site and software company information.)

COMMUNITY RESOURCES

Direct experiences are often the most effective in developing an understanding of a concept. Various community resources, including guest speakers and field trips, can provide useful information and realistic experiences related to various disabilities.

Some communities have hands-on museums that offer students an opportunity to try out a wheelchair on various floor surfaces and experiment with various devices and technology developed to assist those with disabilities. It may also be possible to visit a rehabilitation center.

Guest speakers were suggested for many of the literature selections. In addition to the specialists recommended, parents of children with disabilities and sometimes the children themselves can be wonderful sources of information. "Famous" local people with disabilities may also be invited to talk with the children. These could include school personnel, community professionals, sports figures, and others. Children could hear about how they have adapted to their disabilities and live happy, successful lives.

WRITING

Writing gives children an opportunity to reflect on and respond to what they've listened to or read. A writing response can take various forms—a journal entry written from the perspective of the character with a disability or another character, a poem written about a character or event in the story, a newspaper article reviewing the book, or simply responses to thoughtful questions that can be shared in a discussion.

Writing can be done individually, with a partner, or in small groups. At least initially, the discussion generated in a small group situation may provide new and interesting insights. Children may also want to write their own stories that include someone with a disability. Following editing, their stories could be made into books. Children may enjoy sharing their writing by reading their work to the class, a small group, or a partner. Examples of poetry forms can be found in Appendix A.

RELATED READING

The literature selections in this book include children who have a disability. There are other books that include an adult with a disability. These books may further extend students' understanding. Similar discussion and response activities could be implemented.

Children may also benefit from reading biographies about famous people who happen to have a disability. A musician who is blind, a former president or sports figure who has a learning disabilty, and a television or movie star who has ADHD may provide not only interesting stories, but insights and inspiration to those who have disabilities as well as to those who do not.

New advances in medicine and technology have the power to change the lives of people with disabilities. Reading about and sharing information about these new developments enhance students' awareness. It may be interesting to develop a bulletin board showing past and present ways of dealing with various disabilities.

REFERENCES

Stainback, W., Stainback, S., & Wilkinson, A. (1992). Encouraging peer supports and friendships. *Teaching Exceptional Children*, 24 (2), 6–11.

Surabian, M. (1998). Assistive technology solutions. Paper presented at the Young Adult Institute Annual Conference. April 29, 1998.

Wooten, D. A. The magic of Martin in Culinan, B. E. (1992). *Invitation to read: More children's literature in the reading program*. Newark, DE: International Reading Association.

APPENDIX

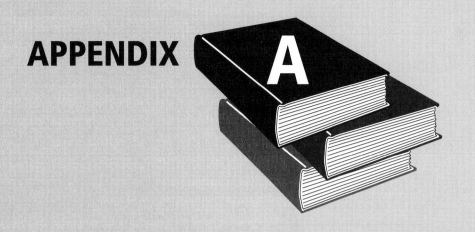

A

POETRY GUIDELINES

ACROSTIC

The topic is written vertically. Words or phrases describing the topic begin with each letter of the topic.

Example:

Bewildered
Like anyone else
Imagine the scene
Not able to see
Dream.

CINQUAIN

Poem of five lines:
Line 1: One word (may be the title)
Line 2: Two words (describing the title)
Line 3: Three words (an action)
Line 4: Four words (a feeling)
Line 5: One word (referring to the title)

Example:

Leukemia

Scary, frightening

Crying in fear

Snuggling with my family

Cancer.

DIAMANTE

(Dee-ah-mahn-tay) is a seven line contrast poem that forms a diamond.
>Line 1: 1 word (noun - subject)
>Line 2: 2 words (adjectives)
>Line 3: 3 words (participles -ing)
>Line 4: 4 words (nouns related to the subject)
>Line 5: 3 words (participles -ing)
>Line 6: 2 words (adjectives)
>Line 7: 1 word (noun - opposite subject)

Example:

Candy
Sweet, delicious
Satisfying my taste
Caramel, chocolate, licorice, mint
Managing to swallow
Fresh, crunchy
Vegetables.

HAIKU

Poem of three lines totaling seventeen syllables.
Line1: 5 syllables
Line 2: 7 syllables
Line 3: 5 syllables

Example:

Children together

Joyful playing and working

Struggle to fit in.

APPENDIX B

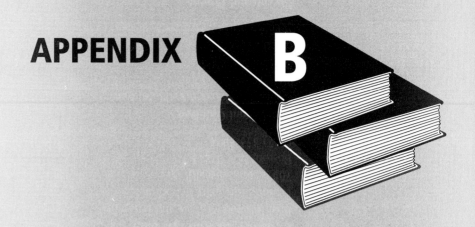

SAMPLE
LESSON PLANS

Although this text reviews books primarily appropriate
for children in the primary grades, lesson plans using
the books can be adapted for students at higher grade levels.

GRADE __3__   **Saint Mary's College**   Lesson Plan No. __2__
Notre Dame, IN

EDUCATION DEPARTMENT

General Subject __reading__   **Name** __Kelli Steenwyk__

Specific Topic __deafness__   **Date** _____

Teacher Objectives	1. Read book: *I Have a Sister, My Sister Is Deaf* and lead discussion on it to increase the understanding and meaning derived from the text. 2. Give quiz to test understanding of concepts explored in lessons about deafness.
Student Objectives	1. Given the book *I Have a Sister, My Sister Is Deaf*, and following discussion, the student will be able to complete a quiz concerning deafness with 80% accuracy or higher. 2. Given the book and discussion, the student will be able to write a page about what they think it would be like to be deaf. The student must include positive and negative aspects and demonstrate knowledge derived from the text and discussion. Writing should also include informed ideas of how to act toward a student who is deaf.
Provisions for varying abilities	1. The text is read orally to eliminate problems with word recognition and other reading problems. 2. The teacher can lead discussion based on how much students seem to be absorbing the information. 3. The student writing can be taken to any level.
Motivation	1. The opportunity to be read aloud to will stimulate some students. 2. The previous activity stimulates student interest in the topic.
Instructional materials needed	- Peterson, Jeanne Whitehouse, *I Have a Sister, My Sister Is Deaf.* Harper & Row: New York, NY (1977). - Quiz on deafness.

Methodologies	**Instructional Activities**
Teacher Strategies	**Expected Student Outcome**

1. Gather students in a circle on the floor. Tell students that you are going to read a story about a girl who is deaf, and that the story is told by her sister. Ask students to pay attention to the methods of communication used by the sisters.	1. Come and sit on the floor, active listening.
2. Read the story, *I Have a Sister, My Sister Is Deaf*.	2. Active listening.
3. Discuss the story with the class. Ask them to tell which forms of communication they noticed. Which aspects of being deaf are handicaps, and which are beneficial? What could the sister do and not do? Tell about famous deaf people, what they could do: Mozart, Helen Keller, etc. What ways is she different, and what ways the same? Does it hurt to be deaf? Can she talk at all? What noises can she 'hear'? Why? Explain why when she says words they sound different than normal. Ask these questions, and discuss any others that come up. Ask the students what they learned.	3. Participate in discussion of the story. Students answer the questions posed by the teacher, and can think of questions on their own. They tell which communication methods they saw, and describe what was learned.
4. Have students write a reflection on the book and about deafness in general. What things are bad, what are good. What is a deaf person like? How should a person treat someone who is deaf? Ask them to write as if they are writing to someone who doesn't know what it is like to be deaf or how to treat a deaf person.	4. Students write personal reflections about what they learned about being deaf from the activity, discussion, and the book.
5. After writing, give students quiz over being deaf. Collect the quiz when finished and go over the answers so children have immediate feedback. Ask for volunteers to offer the answers they gave.	5. Students fill out quiz, hand it in, and go over answers.

GRADE ___2___   **Saint Mary's College**   Lesson Plan No. ___1___
                                  Notre Dame, IN

                           EDUCATION DEPARTMENT

General Subject ___Disabilities - Deafness___   **Name** ___Elisabeth Krick___

Specific Topic ___Reading/Writing___   **Date** _____

Teacher Objectives	Ask students what they think "deaf" means. Read the story, *I Have a Sister, My Sister Is Deaf*, by Jeanne Whitehouse Peterson, out loud. Facilitate a discussion about being deaf and what it means. Divide the class into groups of three or four. Hand out worksheet. Instruct students to list things a person who is deaf can do in one column, and things a person who is deaf cannot do in the other column. Give students time to list several things. Lead a group discussion in which the groups share some of the things they came up with. Ask the students how they could help a person who is deaf with some of the things they cannot do.
Student Objectives	Given the definition for deaf, the student will be able to correctly define "deaf." After listening to the story, *I Have a Sister, My Sister Is Deaf*, the student will be able to share what he or she thinks it means to be deaf. Given a group and a worksheet, the student will be able to work with his or her group to come up with a list of things a person who is deaf can do and a list of things a person who is deaf cannot do. After filling out the worksheet with a group, the student will be able to share some of the things he or she listed. After sharing his or her list, the student will be able to come up with ways that he or she could help people who are deaf with some of the things they cannot do.
Provisions for varying abilities	Reading the story out loud Cooperative group work Discussion
Motivation	A story about a little girl their age Cooperative group work An opportunity to share own ideas
Instructional materials needed	The book, *I Have a Sister, My Sister Is Deaf*, by Jeanne Whitehouse Peterson Worksheet Pencil

Methodologies	**Instructional Activities**
Teacher Strategies	**Expected Student Outcome**
1. Ask the students what they think the word "deaf" means.	1. Volunteer to share what they think "deaf" means.
2. Affirm the correct definition, or, if no one knows, give the definition for "deaf."	2. Actively listen to the story, *I Have a Sister, My Sister Is Deaf.*
3. Read the book, *I Have a Sister, My Sister Is Deaf* out loud to the class.	3. Share what they think it would be like to be deaf.
4. Ask the students questions about what it would be like to be deaf.	4. Fill out the worksheet with as many answers as they can think of in small groups.
5. Divide the class into groups of three or four.	5. Share with the class some ideas the group came up with about things a person who is deaf can and cannot do.
6. Pass out the worksheet, one to each group.	6. Think of ways to help people who are deaf do the things they cannot do.
7. Give instructions: List things a person who is deaf can do in one column, and things a person who is deaf cannot do in the other column.	
8. Give time for students to make lists.	
9. Allow the groups to share with the rest of the class some of the things they came up with.	
10. Ask the students how they could help a person who is deaf with some of the things they cannot do.	

GRADE __2__

Saint Mary's College
Notre Dame, IN

Lesson Plan No. __1__

EDUCATION DEPARTMENT

General Subject __READING__

Name __CHERYL L. WARNER__

Specific Topic __DISABILITIES/WRITING__

Date _____

Teacher Objectives

1. To provide an opportunity for students to experience what others may be feeling through visualization.
2. To promote whole class enrichment for all levels of abilities.
3. To facilitate the opportunity for students to express their emotions through creative writing.
4. To promote understanding of differences.

Student Objectives

After listening to *With the Wind* by Liz Damrell, students will have an interactive class discussion about the feelings of joy, freedom, and how the boy in the story feels.

After the discussion, students will draw a picture about their own feelings. They will be able to accurately describe their picture with a few words or short sentences.

Provisions for varying abilities

The teacher will read in a loud, clear voice and make sure everyone can see the pictures. During the independent writing, the teacher will be accessible to answer questions at all times. The teacher will make any and all accommodations required to keep all students on task.

Motivation

1. Students will listen to a story whose main character is about their own age.
2. The book has beautiful illustrations.
3. The students will be using art supplies.
4. The students will be given freedom of choice.

Instructional materials needed

1. drawing paper
2. pencil
3. markers and/or crayons
4. *With the Wind* by Liz Damrell

Methodologies	Instructional Activities
Teacher Strategies	**Expected Student Outcome**
1. Read *With the Wind* by Liz Damrell.	1. Active listening and looking at pictures.
2. Ask students to identify the boy's disability.	2. Describe the boy's disability.
3. Lead an interactive class discussion about the boy's disability and how he might feel about his limitations.	3. Participate in class discussion.
4. Instruct students to explain the emotions the boy feels while riding.	4. Describe the boy's feelings.
5. State that the boy feels a sense of power and freedom when he is riding the horse. Instruct students to think about something that makes them feel that way and then draw it.	5. Active listening and drawing a picture.
6. Instruct students to write a few words or short sentences to describe their pictures.	6. Write a few words or short sentences to describe their pictures.

GRADE ___1___   **Saint Mary's College**   **Lesson Plan No.** ___2___
Notre Dame, IN

EDUCATION DEPARTMENT

General Subject __Reading/Language Arts__   **Name** __Jean-Marie McMorran__

Specific Topic __Exceptionality- Blindness__   **Date** _____

Teacher Objectives	1. Provide students with a general background about blindness. 2. Read the book *Listen for the Bus, David's Story*, to the class. 3. Discuss blindness in relation to the 5 senses. 4. Initiate discussion about braille and its use. Provide examples and an explanation of the arrangement of the six dot cell to form letters and words. 5. Use braille pattern flash cards to direct class activity. 6. Provide beads for use as raised braille dots for project.
Student Objectives	Using the information provided in the story and the class discussion, students will be able to list the five senses. They will recall in the story how David used taste, touch, smell, and hearing and give an example relating to David's activity. Each student will then tell how he or she uses the senses throughout the day in school. Following a discussion about braille, and using braille flash cards as a guide, the students will be able to write their names using braille symbols. The students will affix beads to represent each raised dot for each letter.
Provisions for varying abilities	Allow ample time for students to record the proper sequence of dots before gluing on the beads. Pre-print each student's name using braille symbols. Allow students with similar letters in their names to work together. If gluing beads is too frustrating, allow student to use a paper punch to punch out the braille letter symbol.
Motivation	The text is written from the perspective of a boy, David, who is close in age to first-grade students. The book contains actual photographs of David and his school; students will enjoy comparing David's day and school to theirs. Students will be interested in feeling braille, and will be curious to create their own form of braille using beads.
Instructional materials needed	*Listen for the Bus, David's Story*, by Patricia McMahon Construction paper, beads, glue, pencil Braille alphabet flash cards Examples of braille writing (optional) . . . examples can be made with glue if none are available

Methodologies	Instructional Activities
Teacher Strategies	**Expected Student Outcome**
1. Ask students if they can name the five senses (sight, taste, touch, smell, hearing). Tell them that when a person loses his or her sense of hearing he or she becomes deaf. Ask what results when a person loses his or her sense of sight . . . (blindness).	1. Students respond to questions. They list the five senses, and identify deafness as a result of losing the sense of hearing . . . most will also identify blindness with the loss of the sense of sight.
2. Introduce the book to the class. Explain to the class that the main character, David, is close to their age. Point out that the book's pictures are real illustrations. Tell students that a photographer probably followed David to school to learn all about his day. Read book.	2. Students listen to the book and observe David's age and surroundings. Most students will identify with David, his school, surroundings, and activities.
3. After story has been read, ask students to recall how David used the senses of taste, smell, touch, and hearing throughout his daily activities (clay, blocks, hammer, swing, bus, locker, rocks, etc.). Ask students to tell how they use each of their senses during school.	3. Students respond to teacher's questions. Some may wish to refer back to the book to find specific examples of how David used 4 of his senses. Most students will readily offer examples of how they use their senses: **sight:** words on chalkboard, **hearing:** lunch/recess bell, **taste:** cafeteria, **touch:** digging in desk to find assignment! **smell:** cafeteria/chalk, dust/animal cages, etc.
4. Begin discussion about braille. Provide students with examples if possible. Explain the six dot configuration used to create each braille letter.	4. Students will feel a braille example and observe the six dots drawn on the board. Students will ask questions for clarification.
5. Show students the braille flash cards. Begin with letter "A"- erase the appropriate dots from the six dot base model drawn on the board to show students how the "A" is drawn. Continue with a few more examples—allow students to come to the board and erase dots to form the letter symbol.	5. Students will view braille flash cards. They will come to the board and erase the appropriate number of dots to correspond with the flash cards.
6. After class understands how braille dots are arranged, pass out construction paper, pencil, and glue. Instruct students to write their first names in capital letters at least 1" high at the bottom edge of the longest side of the paper. (Provide an example or draw on the board.)	6. Students gather supplies, follow teacher's example, and print their names appropriately.

Methodologies	Instructional Activities
Teacher Strategies	**Expected Student Outcome**
7. Show braille flash cards slowly, one at a time to the class. Tell students that when the appropriate letter is shown on the flash cards, they should write its configuration of dots above the corresponding letter in their name. Remind them of the six dot spacing—may be necessary to provide a few more examples on the board.	7. Students draw small circles to copy the dot patterns on the appropriate flash cards that match the letters of their first names. Students may need some letters repeated.
8. Check each students dots to make sure they are as evenly and correctly placed as possible. Distribute a few beads to each student. Instruct them to place a drop of glue on each bead, and then place one bead onto every dot they drew with their pencils.	8. Students use glue and cover each pencil dot with a bead. Each bead represents one raised braille dot.
9. After beads dry, tell students to run their fingers over the beads from left to right. Explain that they have created a larger replica of what their names would feel like if written in braille. Display names on a bulletin board or chalk ledge. Allow students to feel others' names.	9. Students close their eyes and run their hands over the dried beads. Students realize that many people who are blind can read books, music, newspapers, and magazines using the braille system.

GRADE __4,5,6__   **Saint Mary's College**   Lesson Plan No. ____1____
                                   Notre Dame, IN

EDUCATION DEPARTMENT

General Subject Health _____   **Name** __Carrie Ferkenhoff_____

Specific Topic __Learning Disabilities_____   **Date** _____

Teacher Objectives	1. Explain how many famous people have learning disabilities. 2. Promote an understanding of the frustrations that people with learning disabilities experience by reading parts of *The Best Fight*. 3. Promote an understanding of the basic concepts of learning disabilities through lecture and discussion.
Student Objectives	Given a discussion on learning disabilities and the story, *The Best Fight*, the student will be able to write a journal entry about a learning struggle or another type of struggle. The student will include the feelings experienced, what helped him or her through this experience, and how she or he would help someone through a similar struggle.
Provisions for varying abilities	1. Because I am reading this story to the students, those who do have learning disabilities or struggle with reading will not have to focus on decoding the words. Instead, they can give understanding Jamie's feelings about his disability their full attention. 2. In this activity, the students will be given the chance to work in groups as well as work by themselves. During the first part of the lesson, they will imagine what people with learning disabilities must feel like and share their ideas. Toward the end, they will write a journal entry on their own frustrating experience. In this way, both interpersonal and intrapersonal learners will be provided for.
Motivation	1. I will start off this lesson with a discussion about famous people and an interesting question. They will be eager to listen to the story to find out what connection exists between Jamie and well-known people like Tom Cruise and George Bush. 2. Most students, no matter what the grade level, enjoy being read to. The story itself is well written and interesting.
Instructional materials needed	-At least one copy of *The Best Fight* -Paper and pencils or students' journals

Methodologies	Instructional Activities
Teacher Strategies	**Expected Student Outcome**

1. Have the class bring their chairs to the back of the classroom to form a semi-circle around you.	1. Bring your chair to the back of the classroom and form a semi-circle.
2. Ask students what the following people have in common: -American inventor, Thomas Edison -Math genius, Albert Einstein -First woman to reach the North Pole, Ann Bancroft -Presidents, Woodrow Wilson and George Bush -Tom Cruise -Whoopi Goldberg -Cher	2. Guess what the famous people that your teacher names have in common.
3. Tell the class that you are now going to read them a couple of chapters from *The Best Fight*, a story about a boy who has a lot in common with the people we just talked about. Ask the class to listen for the answers to the following questions: -What problem does Jamie experience? -Why do you think Jamie gets into so many fights? -What is Jamie's greatest wish?	3. Listen to your teacher read the story and find out what problem Jamie experiences, why he gets into so many fights, and what he wishes for most.
4. Read the first two chapters of *The Best Fight*. (These chapters show that, although Jamie is in fifth grade, he cannot read. He fights because he is ashamed that he cannot read and is teased by the other kids. His greatest wish is to be able to read adult material and understand grown-up jokes.)	4. Actively listen to the story.
5. Ask the students the questions listed above and discuss the answers.	5. Once the story is finished, try to answer these questions.

Methodologies	Instructional Activities
Teacher Strategies	**Expected Student Outcome**
6. Ask what Jamie and all of the famous people we talked about earlier have in common. Explain that they all struggled with learning disabilities. People thought that Thomas Edison was retarded. Albert Einstein had trouble with arithmetic in school. Ann Bancroft was held back in school because she had trouble learning to read. Woodrow Wilson did not even learn to read until he was eleven.	6. Share what you think Jamie and these famous people have in common.
7. Read excerpts from *The Best Fight* and summarize the conclusion.	7. Listen to the conclusion of *The Best Fight*.
8. Explain that the story about Jamie showed characteristics common to many people with learning disabilities. A person with a learning disability simply has trouble learning something despite being taught well and trying hard to learn. Often such a person struggles in some things, but excels in other things. What did Jamie excel in? Some people compare the way a person with a learning disability thinks with a TV. Some stations are fuzzy, and some are hard to hear, but others come in even stronger and clearer than other TVs. The brains of people with learning disabilities are just too specialized. For example, one girl with a learning disability was an expert at fixing things like bikes and clocks, but she struggled with math. There are many types of learning disabilities. Some people have learning disabilities such as dyslexia. They have difficulty recognizing and reading words. They often learn words by associating them with pictures. Words like "the," "and," and "as" can be confusing since there is no picture to represent them. Other people with learning disabilities have memory problems. They cannot store things in their short-term memories. Often people with learning disabilities feel pretty bad about themselves because teachers, parents, and classmates think they cannot learn	8. Participate in the discussion on learning disabilites.

Methodologies	**Instructional Activities**
Teacher Strategies	**Expected Student Outcome**
because they are stupid or lazy. This is definitely not true. Most likely they are hard workers and very intelligent. Their brains just have to work harder to understand some things. It may take them longer to learn than other students.	
9. Tell the class that, while not everybody experiences learning disabilities, we have all, at some point, had difficulty learning something. Ask the students to write a journal entry on the following topic: 　　—Tell me about a time that you experienced frustrations like Jamie's. How did you feel when you struggled with this? Jamie's principal supported him and helped him realize how much intelligence he had. What helped you get through this? How do you think you could help someone who is going through a struggle like this?	9. Write a journal entry about a struggle you have experienced.
10. Collect students' journal entries.	10. Hand in your journal entry.

GRADE __5__   **Saint Mary's College**   Lesson Plan No. __2__
Notre Dame, IN

EDUCATION DEPARTMENT

General Subject Exceptional Learners   **Name** Laura Kalgren

Specific Topic Disease and disabilities   **Date** _____

Teacher Objectives
To read the story, *Kathy's Hats*, to the group of students.
To have the students engage in the prereading activity of predicting.
To answer any question the group has about disease or disabilities during a group discussion.
For students to understand that being different does not mean we deserve to treat each other badly.
To have the students work on the internet to find more information on cancer.
For students to be aware of the dangers of smoking.

Student Objectives
Given the story, *Kathy's Hats*, the student will be able to ask questions, give opinions, and participate in a discussion about students who have disabilities or illnesses.
Given the correct internet address, the student will explore the American Lung Association Web page, join the smoke free challenge, and participate in the game provided.

Provisions for varying abilities
The students will be in groups.
During the story, students with visual and hearing disabilities will be able to see and hear due to the setting.

Motivation
The students will listen to the story, discuss it, and then have time to explore the topic on the internet. They will be able to sign a pledge to be smoke free.

Instructional materials needed
The book *Kathy's Hats* by Trudy Krisher
Access to computers and internet
Internet address for the American Cancer Society:
http://www.cancer.org/smokeout/

Methodologies	Instructional Activities
Teacher Strategies	**Expected Student Outcome**
1. Gather a group of 10 students.	1. The students will gather.
2. Have the students arrange their chairs in a circle around the table.	2. The students will make a circle around the table with their chairs.
3. Show cover of book, read title, and ask students to predict the story.	3. The students will make predictions about the story.
4. Begin reading the story, *Kathy's Hats*, to the group.	4. The students will listen to the story being read and look at the pictures.
5. Finish the story—let the students react to what they heard.	5. The students will react to the story by talking to one another and asking questions.
6. Go back through the story, answering the questions the students may ask about the story or cancer.	6. The students will ask questions relating to the story or the disease.
7. Ask the students questions: -How many types of hats did Kathy wear? -What was special about her last hat? -Why did Kathy have to wear a hat?	7. The students will respond to the questions asked by the teacher.
8. Continue discussion about the story and how Kathy may have felt or how her classmates may have felt.	8. Students will participate in the discussion by asking questions or giving input, sharing stories, or opinions.
9. Open the discussion to include students with disabilities or students who are "different."	9. Students will participate in the discussion by asking questions or giving input, sharing stories, or opinions.
10. Take the students to the library to use the computers.	10. Students will follow teacher to the library.
11. Explain how and help them access the internet. Once in the internet ask them to go to: **http://www.cancer.org/smokeout/**	11. Students will listen to directions and then access the internet, go to the address given.
12. Explain that the site they are looking at is from the American Cancer Society and there is information explaining what the group has been talking about.	12. Students will listen to the teacher's explanation of what this site is about.

Methodologies	Instructional Activities
Teacher Strategies	**Expected Student Outcome**
13. Let the students explore the site, encourage them to play the games, *The Underground and Life L"IKE."*	13. Students will explore and find information about cancer, play the games, *The Underground and Life L"IKE."*
14. Have the students sign and print out their smoke free pledge and print out the pictures they have made.	14. The students will sign the smoke free pledge and print out a copy. They will also print out a copy of the pictures they created from the games.
15. When it is time to leave, have the students exit the internet.	15. The students will go off line.

APPENDIX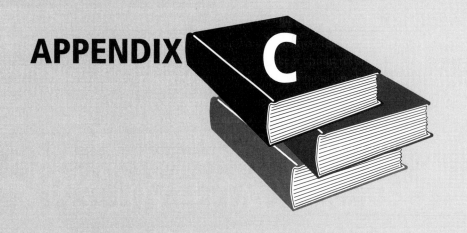

ORGANIZATIONS

Please note that because internet resources are of a time-sensitive nature and URL addresses may change or be deleted, searches should also be conducted by association and/or topic.

GENERAL

ADA Disabilities Information Line
U.S. Dept. of Justice
Civil Rights Division, Disabilities Rights Section
Box 66730
Washington, DC 20035-66738
(800) 514-0301
Web site: http://www.asdoj.gov/crt/ada/

Alliance for Technology Access
2175 E. Francisco Blvd., Suite L
San Rafael, CA 94901
(415) 455-4575
E-mail: atainfo@ataccess.org
Web site: http://www.ataccess.org/ataccess/

The Arc of the United States
500 E. Border St., Suite 300
Arlington, TX 76010
(817) 261-6003
E-mail: thearc@metronet.com
Web site: http://www.TheArc.org/welcome.html

Beach Center on Families and Disability
University of Kansas
3111 Haworth Hall
Lawrence, KS 66045
(785) 864-7600
E-mail: beach@dole.lsi.ukans.edu

Center for Innovations in Special Education
Parkade Center, Suite 152
601 Business Loop 70 West
Columbia, MO 65211
Web site: http://www.tiger.coe.missouri.edu/-mocise
Publications must be ordered from the Instructional Materials Laboratory of
University of Missouri, Columbia - Phone (800) 669-2465

Children's Defense Fund
25 E St., NW
Washington, DC 20001
(202) 662-3652
E-mail: http://www.childrensdefense.org

Consortium on Inclusive Schooling Practices
Child and Family Studies Program
Allegheny-Singer Research Institute
320 E. North Ave.
Pittsburgh, PA 15212
Web site: http://www.asri.edu/CFSP brochure/abtcons.htm

Council for Exceptional Children
1920 Association Dr.
Reston, VA 22091
(703) 620-3660
Web site: http://www.sped.org

DREAMMS for Kids, Inc.
273 Ringwood Rd.
Freeville, NY 13068-9618
(607) 529-3027
E-mail: DREAMMS@aol.com
Web site: http://www.users.aol.com/dreamms/

Institute on Disability UAP
University of New Hampshire
7 Leavitt Lane, Suite 101
Durham, NH 03824-3522
(603) 862-4320
E-mail: institute disability@unh.edu
Web site: http://www.iod.unh.edu

March of Dimes
Resource Center
1275 Mamaroneck Ave.
White Plains, NY 10605
(888) MODIMES; (914) 997-4764 TTY
Web site: http://www.modimes.org

National Center for Youth with Disabilities
University of Minnesota, Box 722
420 Delaware St., SE
Minneapolis, MN 55455-0392
(612) 626-2825 / (800) 333-6293
E-mail: ncyd@gold.tc.umn.edu
Web site: http://www.peds.umn.edu.Centers/ncyd

National Information Center for Children and Youth with Disabilities (NICHCY)
P.O. Box 1492
Washington, DC 20013-1492
(800) 695-0285
E-mail: nichcy@aed.org
Web site: http://www.nichcy.org

National Organization on Disability
910 16th St., NW
Washington, DC 20006
(202) 293-5960
Web site: http://www.nod.org

The National Rehabilitation Information Center (NARIC)
8455 Colesville Rd.
Suite 935
Silver Spring, MD 20910-3319
(800) 346-2742 / (301) 588-9284
Web site: http://www.naric.com/naric

National Easter Seal Society
230 W. Monroe St., Suite 1800
Chicago, IL 60606-4802
(312) 726-6200
Web site: http://www.seals.com

National Library Service for the Blind and Physically Handicapped
Library of Congress
1291 Taylor St. NW
Washington, DC 20542
(800) 424-8567
E-mail: nls@loc.gov
Web site: http://www.loc.gov/nls

North American Riding for the Handicapped Association (NHRHA)
P.O. Box 33150
Denver, CO 80233
(303) 452-1212 / (800) 369-7433

Sibling Information Network
University of Connecticut
A. J. Pappanikou Center
249 Glenbrook Rd., U-64
Storrs, CT 06269-2064
(860) 486-4985

Sibling Support Project
Children's Hospital and Medical Center
P.O. Box 5371, CL-09
Seattle, WA 98105
(206) 368-4911
E-mail: dmeyer@chmc.org
Web site: http://www.chmc.org.departmt/sibsupp

Very Special Arts
1300 Connecticut Ave., NW
Washington, DC 20036
(202) 628-2800

SPECIFIC DISABILITIES

Aids

CDC National AIDS Clearinghouse
P.O. Box 6003
Rockville, MD 20849-6003
(800) 458-5231

National Pediatric HIV Resource Center
15 South Ninth St.
Newark, NJ 07107
(210) 268-8251

Attention Deficit Disorder

Children and Adults with Attention Deficit Disorder (CH.A.D.D.)
499 Northwest 70th Ave., Suite 109
Plantation, FL 33317
(305) 587-3700
Web site: http://www.chadd.org/

Attention Deficit Disorder Association (ADDA)
P.O. Box 972
Mentor, OH 44061
(800) 487-2282

Autism

Autism Network International (ANI)
P.O. Box 448
Syracuse, NY 13210-0448
E-mail: bordner@uiuc.edu
Web site: http://www.students.uiuc.edu/-bordner/nai.html

Autism Services Center (ASC)
Pritchard Building
605 9th Street
P.O. Box 507
Huntington, WV 25710-0507
(304) 525-8026

Autism Society of America (ASA)
7910 Woodmont Ave., Suite 650
Bethesda, MD 20814
(800) 328-8476
Web site: http/www.autism-society.org/

Center for Study of Autism
9725 SW Beaverton-Hillsdale Highway, Suite 230
Beaverton, OR 97005

Future Horizons
422 E. Lamar, Suite 106
Arlington, TX 76011
(800) 489-0727

TEACCH Division
Administration & Research
CB # 7180, Medical School Wing E
University of North Carolina at Chapel Hill
Chapel Hill, NC 27599-7180
(919) 966-2174

Cancer

Candlelighters Childhood Cancer Foundation
7910 Woodmont Ave., Suite 460
Bethesda, MD 20814
(301) 657-8401

National Cancer Information Service
Office of Cancer Communications
Building 31, Room 10A16
31 Center Dr., MSC 2580
Bethesda, MD 20892

Cerebral Palsy

March of Dimes
Resource Center
1275 Mamaroneck Ave.
White Plains, NY 10605
(888) MODIMES
Web site: http://www.modimes.org

United Cerebral Palsy (UCP)
1660 L St., N.W., Suite 700
Washington, DC 20036
(800) 872-5827
Web site: http://www.ucpa.org

Deafness and Hearing Loss

Alexander Graham Bell Association for the Deaf
3417 Volta Place, NW
Washington, DC 20007-2778
(202) 337-5220
E-mail: agbell2@aol.com
Web site: http://www.agbell.org

American Society for Deaf Children
1820 Tribute Rd., Suite A
Sacramento, CA 95815
(800) 942-2732
E-mail: asdcl@aol.com
Web site: http://www.edu.kent.edu/deaf/asdchome.html

Beginnings for Parents of Hearing Impaired Children
3900 Barrett Dr., Suite 100
Raleigh, NC 27609
(800) 541-4327

John Tracy Clinic
806 W. Adams Blvd.
Los Angeles, CA 90007
(800) 522-4582

Meniere's Network
The Ear Foundation
1817 Patterson St.
Nashville, TN 37203
(800) 545-4327 / (615) 329-7807

National Association of the Deaf
814 Thayer Ave.
Silver Spring, MD 20910
(301) 587-1788
E-mail: NADHQ@juno.com
Web site: http://www.nad.org

National Information Center on Deafness
Gallaudet University
800 Florida Ave., NE
Washington, DC 20002-3695
(202) 651-5051
E-mail: nicd@gallux.gallaudet.edu/-nicd

TRIPOD
2901 N. Keystone St.
Burbank, CA 91504-1620
(818) 972-2080 / (818) 972-2090

Diabetes

American Diabetes Association
National Service Center
18 East 48th St.
New York, NY 10017
(800) 232-3472

Juvenile Diabetes Foundation International
432 Park Ave. South, 16th Floor
New York, NY 10016
(800) 533-2873

Down Syndrome

Association for Children with Down Syndrome
2616 Martin Ave.
Bellmore, NY 11710
(516) 221-4700
E-mail: info@acds.org
Web site: http://www.acds/org

National Association for Down Syndrome (NADS)
P.O. Box 4542
Oak Brook, IL 60522-4542
(708) 325-9112
Web site: http://www.nads.org/

National Down Syndrome Congress (NDSC)
1605 Chantilly Dr. Suite 250
Atlanta, GA 30324
(800) 222-NDSC
E-mail: NDSCcenter@aol.com
Web site: http://www.carol.net/-ndsc

National Down Syndrome Society (NDSS)
666 Broadway
New York, NY 10012-2317
(212) 460-9330 / (800) 221-4602
Web site: http://www.ndss.org/

Emotional and Behavioral Disorders

The Federation of Families for Children's Mental Health
1021 Prince St.
Alexandria, VA 22341-2971
(703) 684-7710

National Clearinghouse on Family Support and Children's Mental Health
P.O. Box 751
Portland, OR 97207-0751
(800) 628-1696

Epilepsy

American Epilepsy Society
638 Prospect Ave.
Hartford, CT 06105-4250
(203) 586-7505
E-mail: aesmain@aol.com

Epilepsy Canada
1470 Peel St., Suite 745
Montreal, Quebec H3A 1T1
Canada
(514) 845-7855

Epilepsy Foundation of America
4351 Garden City Dr.
Landover, MD 20785-2267
(800) EFA-1000; (800) 332-2070 (TTY)
E-mail: postmaster@efa.org
Web site: http://www.efa.org

Fetal Alcohol Syndrome

Fetal Alcohol Syndrome Family Resource Institute
P.O. Box 2525
Lynnwood, WA 98036
(425) 778-4048

The National Organization on Fetal Alcohol Syndrome (NOFAS)
1815 H St., NW, Suite 1000
Washington, DC 20006
(800) 66-NOFAS

Hydrocephalus

Hydrocephalus Association
870 Market St., Suite 955
San Francisco, CA 94102
(415) 732-7040
Web site: http://www.neurosurgery.mgh.harvard.edu/ha/

Learning Disabilities

Learning Disabilities Association of America
4156 Library Road
Pittsburgh, PA 15234
(412) 341-1515
E-mail: ldanatl@usaor.net
Web site: http://www.ldanatl.org

National Center for Learning Disabilities
381 Park Ave. South, Suite 1240
New York, NY 10016
(212) 545-7510

The Orton Dyslexia Society
Chester Building, Suite 382
8600 LaSalle Rd.
Baltimore, MD 21286-2044
(800) ABCD123
E-mail: info@ods.org
Web site: http://www.ods.org

Mental Retardation

American Association on Mental Retardation
444 N. Capitol St., NW, Suite 846
Washington, DC 20001-1512
(800) 424- 3688 / (202) 387-1968
E-mail: AAMR@access.digex.net

Council for Exceptional Children
Division on Mental Retardation and Developmental Disabilities
1920 Association Dr.
Reston, VA 20191-1589
(703) 620-3660 / (800) 845-6232
Web site: http://www.cec.sped.org

TASH
29 W. Susquehanna Ave., Suite 210
Baltimore, MD 21204
(410) 828-6706

Muscular Dystrophy

Muscular Dystrophy Association
3300 E. Sunrise Dr.
Tucson, AZ 85718
(520) 529-2000
Web site: http://www.mdausa.org

Society for Muscular Dystrophy Information International
P.O. Box 479
Bridgewater, Nova Scotia B4V 2X6
Canada
(902) 682-3086

Physical Disabilities

The Center for Universal Design
North Carolina State University
School of Design
P.O. Box 850
Rocklin, CA 95677
(916) 632-0922

National Easter Seal Society
230 W. Monroe St., Suite 1800
Chicago, IL 60606-4802
(312) 726-6200
Web site: http://www.seals.com

Speech and Language Disorders

American Speech Language Hearing Association (ASHA)
10801 Rockville Pike
Rockville, MD 20822
(800) 638-8255 (VTTY)
Web site: http://www.asha.org

National Institute on Deafness and Other Communication Disorders
1 Communication Ave.
Bethesda, MD 20892-3456
(800) 241-1044 / (800) 241-1055 (TTY)
E-mail: nidcd@aerie.com
Web site: http://www.nih.gov/nidcd/

Stuttering Foundation of America
P.O. Box 11749
Memphis, TN 38111-0749
(800) 992-9392 / (901) 452-7343

Trace Research and Development Center
University of Wisconsin—Madison
S-151 Waisman Center
1500 Highland Ave.
Madison, WI 53705-2280
(603) 262-6966
E-mail: info@trace.wise.edu
Web site: http://www.trace.wise.edu

The United States Society for Augmentative and Alternative Communication (USSAAC)
P.O. Box 5271
Evanston, IL 60204-5271
(847) 869-2122

Spina Bifida

March of Dimes
Resource Center
1275 Mamaroneck Ave.
White Plains, NY 10605
(888) MODIMES / (914) 997-4764 (TTY)

National Information Center for Children and Youth with Disabilities (NICHCY)
P.O. Box 1492
Washington, DC 20013-1492
(800) 695-0285
E-mail: nichcy@aed.org
Web site: http://www.nichcy.org

Spina Bifida Association of America
4590 MacArthur Blvd., NW, Suite 250
Washington, DC 20007-4226
(800) 621-3141 / (202) 944-3285

Spina Bifida Association of Canada
220-388 Donald St.
Winnipeg, Manitoba R3B 2J4
Canada
(204) 957-1784
E-mail: spinab@mts.net

Spinal Cord Injury

American Paralysis Association
500 Morris Ave.
Springfield, NJ 07081
(800) 225-0292
Web site: http://www.apa.uci.edu/paralysis

National Spinal Cord Injury Association
8300 Colesville Rd., Suite 551
Silver Spring, MD 20910
(800) 962-9629 Hotline / 301) 588-6959
Web site: http://www.trader.com/users/5010/1020/nscia.htm

National Spinal Cord Injury Hotline
2201 Argonne Dr.
Baltimore, MD 21218
(800) 526-3456

Spinal Network
23815 Stuart Ranch Rd.
Malibu, CA 90265
(800) 543-4116

Tourette Syndrome

Tourette Syndrome Association
42-40 Bell Blvd.
Bayside, NY 11361-2820
(718) 224-2999

Tourette Syndrome Foundation of Canada
238 Davenport Rd., Box 343
Toronto, Ontario M5R 1J6
Canada
(416) 636-2800

Traumatic Brain Injury

Brain Injury Association
1776 Massachusetts Ave., NW, Suite 100
Washington, DC 20036-1904
(202) 296-6443 / (800) 440-6443 Family Helpline
Web site: http://www.biausa.org

Visual Impairment and Blindness

American Council of the Blind
1155 15th St. NW, Suite 720
Washington, DC 20005
(202) 467-5081 / (800) 424-8666

American Foundation for the Blind
11 Penn Plaza, Suite 300
New York, NY 10001
(404) 525-2303 / (800) AFB-LINE
E-mail: afbinfo@afb.org
Web site: http://www.afb.org/afb/

Blind Children's Center
4120 Marathon St.
Los Angeles, CA 90029
(213) 664-2153 / (800)222-3567 (CA) / (800) 222-3566 (U.S.)
E-mail: info@blindcntr.org
Web site: http://www.blindcntr.org/bcc

National Association for Visually Handicapped
22 West 21st St.
New York, NY 10010
(212) 889-3141
Web site: http://www.navh.org

National Federation of the Blind
1800 Johnson St.
Baltimore, MD 21230
(410) 659-9314

APPENDIX D

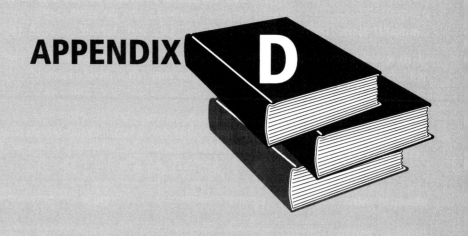

PERIODICALS

GENERAL

The Americans with Disabilities Newsletter
P.O. Box 365
Hillsdale, NY 12529-0365
(800) 818-3111

Children's Software Review
44 Main St.
Flemington, NJ 08822
(800) 993-9499

Closing the Gap
P.O. Box 68
Henderson, MN 56044
(612) 248-3294

Disability Advocates Bulletin
Pike Institute on Law and Disability
Boston University School of Law
765 Commonwealth Ave.
Boston, MA 02215
(617) 353-2904

Exceptional Children
Council for Exceptional Children
1920 Association Dr.
Reston, VA 22091
(888) 222-7733
Web site: http://www.cec.spec.org.

Exceptional Parent
P.O. Box 3000, Dept. EP
Denville, NJ 07834
(800) 562-1973
Web site: http://www.familyeducation.com

Families and Disability Newsletter
Beach Center on Families and Disability
University of Kansas
3111 Haworth Hall
Lawrence, KS 66045
(785) 864-7600

Inclusion News
Inclusion Press International
24 Thome Crescent
Toronto, Ontario, M6H 2S5
Canada
(416) 658-5363
Web site: http://www.inclusion.com

SPEAK OUT
PEAK Parent Center, Inc.
6055 Lehmann Dr., Suite 101
Colorado Springs, CO 80918
(719) 531-9400

Technology and Inclusion News
Box 12109
Austin, TX 78709
(512) 280-7235

Tuesday's Child
P.O. Box 270046
Ft. Collins, CO
(970) 416-7416
E-mail: tueskid@frii.com

SPECIFIC DISABILITIES

Attention Deficit Disorder

Brakes: The Interactive Newsletter for Kids with ADD
ADD WareHouse
300 NW 70th Ave., Suite 102
Plantation, FL 33317
(800) 233-9273 / (954) 792-8545

Deafness and Hearing Loss

Silent News
133 Gaither Dr., Suite E.
Mount Laurel, NJ 08054-1710

Down Syndrome

Communicating Together
P.O. Box 6395
Columbia, MD 21045-6395
(410) 995-0722

Disability Solutions
9220 SW Barbur Blvd., #119-179
Portland, OR 97219-5428
E-mail:dsolns@teleport.com

Hydrocephalus

Hydrocephalus News & Notes
National Hydrocephalus Foundation
1670 Green Oak Circle
Lawrenceville, GA 30243

Hydrocephalus Newsletter
Hydrocephalus Association
870 Market St., Suite 955
San Francisco, CA 94102
(415) 732-7040

REFERENCES

Meyer, D. and Vadasy, P. (1996). *Living with a Brother or Sister with Special Needs: A Book for Sibs*. Seattle: University of Washington Press.

Sweeney, W. K. (1998). *The Special-Needs Reading List*. Bethesda, MD: Woodbine House.

APPENDIX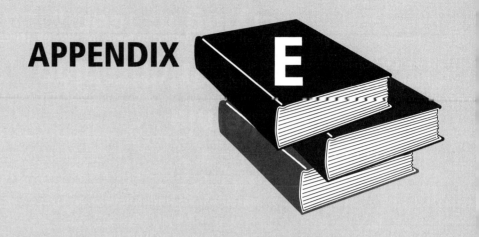

WEB SITES

WEB SITE ADDRESSES

Please note that because internet resources are of a time-sensitive nature and URL addresses may change or be deleted, searches should also be conducted by association and/or topic.

http://www.abledata.com/index.htm
ABLEDATA is an electronic database of information on assistive technology and rehabilitation equipment available in the United States. With more than 23,000 product listings, ABLEDATA covers everything from white canes and adaptive clothing to low vision reading systems and voice output programs. Each product record provides a detailed description of the item, complete company contact information, and distributor listings (where applicable). In addition to commercially available products, the database also lists noncommercial prototypes, customized products, and one-of-a-kind products.

http://www.ics.forth.gr/proj/rti/
Assistive Tech and Human Computer Interaction Lab.

http://www.access.digex.net/~edlawinc/
Edlaw
Information on the Individuals with Disabilities Education Act (IDEA) and Section 504 of the Rehabilitation Act, links to disability law on the Internet. This page should provide a starting point for basic legal information of use to special educators, parents, and their advisors in meeting federal and state requirements for the education of students with disabilities.

http://www.zdnet.com/yil/content/growth/soclserv/dsbl1.html
Yahoo Disability - Related Resources.

http://www.primes6.rehab.uiuc.edu:80/pursuit/homepage.html
Here you will find a wealth of resources, including disability information, education accommodation resources, lessons on assistive technology and funding available for this technology, descriptions of careers in science, engineering, and mathematics, high school preparations for these careers, and access to countless other disability information servers.

http://www.assisttech.com/
AssisTech Inc.: low-cost, mainstream, technology solutions. Focused on challenges faced by persons with disabilities and their families.

http://www.inform.umd.edu/EdRes/Topic/Disability/
Disability Directory: The Disability Directory is a combination of newsletters, articles, resource guides, current laws, and upcoming conventions that benefit those who are physically impaired.

http://www.discovertechnology.com/DisDirectory.html
Resource for links to sites that are specifically geared toward persons with disabilities and with special interest in adaptive technology.

http://www.inform.umd.edu/edRes/Topic/Disability/InternetRes/ WWWAccess/
World Wide Web Access Pages on Disability Resources.

http://www.specialed.miningco.com/
Internet resources for special educators.

http://www.janweb.icdi.wvu.edu/links/disspec.htm
This page contains web resources categorized by disability.

http://www.yahoo.com/Society and Culture/Disabilities/
Offers links to various web sites re: Disabilities.

http://www.ablelink.org/
Ability OnLine is an electronic mail system that connects young people with disabilities or chronic illness to peers and mentors with and without disabilities.

http://www.asel.udel.edu/at-online/
Assistive Tech On-Line.

http://www.dreamms.org/
DREAMMS for Kids, Inc.: An assistive technology information clearinghouse.

Founded by the parents of a child with Down syndrome, DREAMMS is committed to increasing the use of computers, high-quality instructional technology, and assistive technologies for students with special needs in schools, homes and the workplace. Programs and services are specially designed to assist parents and teachers in their search for technology-based solutions for the kids in their care.

http://www.nls.org/
Neighborhood Legal Services, Inc. NLS provides free legal services to persons with low income and persons with disabilities. It also provides a wide range of technical assistance and support services, primarily under its disability-related grants, and operates both a statewide and national Assistive Technology Advocacy Project to assist persons with disabilities, and the advocates and agencies that serve them.

http://indie.ca/about.cfm?language=English&Mode=Gfx
Indie: A leading information directory of disability resources, comprehensive one-stop resource for products, services, and information for the worldwide disability community.

http://inclusion.com
Inclusion Press International

APPENDIX F

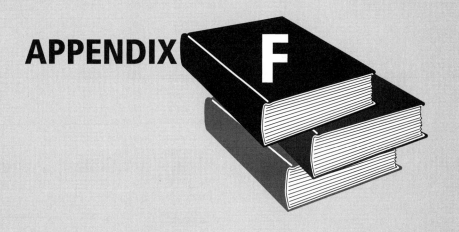

PUBLISHER ADDRESSES

Alfred A. Knopf
Division of Random House
Peter Jansen
201 East 50th St.
New York, NY 10022

Albert Whitman & Company
6340 Oakton St.
Morton Grove, IL 60053

Beacon Press
Division of Random House
25 Beacon St.
Boston, MA 02108

Behavioral Publications
Division of Behaviorial Therapy Institute
710 Old Mill Rd
San Marino, CA 91108

Carolrhoda Books, Inc.
Affiliation of The Lerner Group
241 First Ave., N.
Minneapolis, MN 55401

Checkerboard Press
1560 Revere Rd.
Yardley, PA 19067

Children's Press
Div. of Grolier, Inc.
90 Sherman Turnpike
Danbury, CT 06816

Clarion Books
c/o Houghton Mifflin Trade Books
215 Park Ave. S.
New York, NY 10003

Coward-McCann
The Putnam Publishing Group
200 Madison Ave.
New York, NY 10016

Crown Publishing, Co.
P.O. Box 1337
Santa Clarita, CA 91386

Current, Inc.
P.O.Box 2559
Colorado Springs, CO 80901

Deaconess Press
Division of Fairview Press
2450 Riverside Ave., S.
Minneapolis, MN 55454

Delmar/Thomson Learning
3 Columbia Circle, Box 15015
Albany, NY 12212-5015

Dial Books
Division of Dell Publishing Co.
Division of Bantam Doubleday Dell
1540 Broadway
New York, NY 10036

Dial Books for Young Readers
375 Hudson St.
New York, NY 10014

Dilligaf Publishing
64 Court St.
Ellsworth, ME 04605

Dillon
Subs. of Harold Dillon, Inc.
460 S. Marion Parkway Apt. 851B
Denver, CO 80209

Farrar, Straus & Giroux
Desk Copy Request Contact:
Kelli McMahon
Farrar, Straus & Giroux
19 Union Square West
New York, NY 10003

Four Winds Press
265 Tenafly Rd.
Tenafly, NJ 07670

Franklin Watts
Division of Grolier, Inc.
Sherman Turnpike
Danbury, CT 06813

Friendship Press
475 Riverside Dr., Room 860
New York, NY 10115

Gareth Stevens Children's Books
River Ctr. Bldg
1555 N. River Center Dr. Suite 201
Milwaukee, WI 53212

Gemma B. Publishing, Inc.
Box 713-740 Corydon Ave.
Winnipeg, Manitoba, R3M 0YI
Canada

Greenwillow Books
Division of William Morrow & Co., Inc.
1350 Ave. of the Americas
New York, NY 10019

GSI Publications
P.O. Box 746
DeWitt, NY 13214

Harcourt Brace Co.
6277 Sea Harbor Dr.
Orlando, FL 32887

Herald Press
616 Walnut Ave.
Scottdale, PA 15683

Holiday House Books
425 Madison Ave.
New York, NY 10017

Holt, Henry & Company
123 W. 18th St., 5th floor
New York, NY 10011

Holt, Rinehart & Winston
1120 S. Capital of Texas Highway NoII-100
Austin, TX 78746

Houghton Mifflin Company
215 Park Ave. S.
New York, NY 10003

Human Sciences Press
Subs. of Plenum Publishing Corp.
233 Spring St.
New York, NY 10013

Ideals Children's Books
Division Hambleton-Hill Publishing, Inc.
1501 County Hospital Rd
Nashville, TN 37218

Jason and Nordic Publishers
P.O. Box 441
Hollidaysburg, PA 16648

Lippincott-Raven
Subs. of Wolters Kluwer US Corp.
227 E. Washington Sq.
Philadelphia, PA 19106

Julian Messner
299 Jefferson Rd.
Parsippany, NJ 07054

Lerner Publications
241 First Ave. North
Minneapolis, MN 55401

Little, Brown & Company
3 Center Plaza
Boston, MA 02108

Lothrop, Lee & Shepard Books
1350 Avenue of the Americas
New York, NY 10019

Macmillan Publishing USA
201 W. 103rd St.
Indianapolis, IN 46290

Magination Press
Contact American Psychological Association
c/o APA Books
750 1st St. NE
Washington, DC 20002

McGraw-Hill Publishing
860 Taylor Station Rd.
Blacklick, OH 43004

Orchard Books
95 Madison Ave. 7th floor
New York, NY 10016

Paulist Press
Desk Copy Request Contact:
Carol Lally
997 MacArthur Blvd.
Mahwah, NJ 07430

Penguin Books USA
375 Hudson St. 4th Fl.
New York, NY 10014

Prentice Hall
Prentice Hall and Professional Technical
Reference: Faculty Services Dept.
One Lake St.
Upper Saddle River, NJ 07458

Random House
201 E. 50th Street
New York, NY 10022

Real Life Storybooks
8370 Kentland Ave.
West Hills, CA 91304

Simon & Schuster, Inc.
200 Old Tappan Rd.
Old Tappan, NJ 07675

Sopris West
4093 Specialty Place
Longmont, CO 80504

Tim Peters and Co.
87 Main St.
Peapack, NJ 07977

Verbal Images Press
19 Fox Hill Dr.
Fairport, NY 14450

Wadsworth Publishing Co.
10 Davis Drive
Belmont, CA 94002

Walker & Company
435 Hudson St.
New York, NY 10014

Waterfront Books
85 Crescent Rd.
Burlington, VT 05401

Windswept House
P.O. Box 159
Mt. Desert, ME 04660

Woodbine House
6510 Bells Mill Rd.
Bethesda, MD 20817

Writer's Press
2309 Mountainview Dr. Suite 190
Boise, ID 83706

INDEX